THE ADDER'S DEN;

OR SECRETS OF THE

GREAT CONSPIRACY

TO OVERTHROW LIBERTY IN AMERICA.

DEPRAVITY OF SLAVERY:

TWO PRESIDENTS SECRETLY ASSASSINATED BY POISON.

UNSUCCESSFUL ATTEMPTS TO MURDER THREE OTHERS.—THE EVIDENCE CONCLUSIVE, AND THE FACTS ESTABLISHED. TOGETHER WITH THE DYING STRUGGLES OF THE

GREAT SOUTHERN REBLLION.

BY JOHN SMITH DYE.

NEW YORK:
PUBLISHED BY THE AUTHOR,
No. 32 BEEKMAN STREET.—Post Office Box, 5,750.
1864.

Entered according to Act of Congress, in the year 1864, by

JOHN SMITH DYE,

In the Clerk's Office of the District Court of the United States, for the Southern District of New York.

F. SOMERS, Printer and Stereotyper,
32 Beekman St., N. Y.

THE FATHERS

OF

THE REVOLUTION.

THEIR DEVOTION TO FREEDOM.

On the fifteenth day of May, 1776, the birds had returned with the season, and were making forest and grove resound with their songs. The beautiful spring flowers had matured in all their loveliness, and climbing on their tiny leaves the Honey Bee sweetly sung out that winter was gone.

Although nature was smiling, the Colonies were sad. The tyranny of England had kindled a feeling of revenge in their minds, which soon cast the political elements back into chaos. It was on the above mentioned day, that John Adams, as Chairman of a Committee, presented a resolution in Congress, which was adopted, recommending to the respected assemblage and convention of the United Colonies, the establishment of a government suited to the exigency of the times. This resolution gained favor with the public, and on the seventeenth day of June following, Richard Henry Lee moved, and John Adams seconded the resolution, declaring that "these United Colonies are, and of right ought to be, free and independent States; and that all political connection between them and Great Britain is, and ought to be, totally dissolved." After daily deliberations on these resolutions for over a month, on the second of July they were unanimously adopted by Congress; and on the same day it appointed THOMAS JEFFERSOM, JOHN

ADAMS, BENJAMIN FRANKLIN, ROGER SHERMAN and ROBERT R. LIVINGSTON a Committee to draft "a Declaration of Independence."

Although Mr. Adams was rocked in the cradle of liberty, Mr. Jefferson was unanimously known as her champion; and on him was the honor conferred of drafting the Declaration. He did it; and, after some amendments, it was solemnly adopted in the city of Philadelphia, on the glorious and ever memorable Fourth of July, 1776. After being read, the great bell on the hall began, as if by magic, to ring, reverberating the great and immortal truths just promulgated. Its loud notes thundered dismay to the minds of tyrants, but kindled hope in the breasts of the people.

The enemy having a large naval force in our harbors, savages on our frontiers, treason in our camps, spies in our cities, gold in their coffers, and gibbets in their eye—the fawning sycophant, the man who wanted peace in his day, the go-between threatening and promising; and last, the cowardly sympathizer with the hated foe—all these to other men would have appeared unsurmountable obstacles. But in the face of all—God bless them—they boldly stepped forward, determined to be free, leaving themselves no alternative but "liberty or death."

They had the sagacity to determine the right, and the courage to maintain it. While others were wavering, they were firm; they could neither be courted, intimidated nor bribed; the wealth of the Indies would have been to them as dust. No royal standard could have induced them to forsake the standard of liberty. In the darkest hour a halo of glory surrounded them—a secret self-sustaining influence, which dispelled all gloom. They gathered from the never changing laws of human nature, that mankind, without regard to race, condition, country, clime or color. desired and deserved every where to be free.

Thus, "life, liberty, and the pursuit of happiness" are enunciated in the Declaration of Independence as the inherent rights of man; "and to secure these rights governments are instituted among men, deriving their just power from the consent of the governed."

Here Mr. Jefferson not only sets forth and enumerated the rights, but he positively asserts that to secure them is the chief object of governments. He discards the idea of governing by "divine right," and shows that governments should be created, not against, but by the will and consent of the governed. The power to rule is always lodged with the people, and put in motion by the will of the majority.

This was the foundation laid down in the Bill of Rights; and wherever it has been steadily adhered to, liberty has been protected, life has been secure, property well guarded, and unbounded prosperity has everywhere been the reward, to such a degree that it has no parallel in the history of mankind. God, in his infinite wisdom, decreed that the man who wrote the Declaration, and the man who advocated it, were the last living witnesses of its adoption by the American Congress, and the latest survivors of those who subscribed it on the Fourth of July. Charles Carroll, being absent on a secret mission on the fourth, subscribed it afterwards.

On the anniversary of the fiftieth year from the day the Declaration of Independence was adopted, they both departed this life. When the sun of the glorious Jubilee shone in unclouded and meridian splendor, during the very hour on which, fifty years before, the Declaration was read by him and adopted by Congress, THOMAS JEFFERSON died, exulting that that was the day and the hour. Just as the sun was saluting with his parting rays the same glorious day, and during the very hour on which, fifty years before, the Declaration of Independence was read from the State House to the citizens of Philadelphia, JOHN ADAMS expired, exclaiming, "It is a great and glorious day;" and while giving utterance to the last word he departed.

These great men always understood the design and end of government to be *freedom* and *security*. And however our eyes may be beguiled with show, or our ears deceived by sound; however prejudice may warp our judgments, or interest darken our understandings, the simple voice of nature and reason will say it is right.

They had no model in Grecian or Roman history to build from; but took as their guide the desire of all men to be free. Liberty was the chief corner-stone; they claimed it as a gift from the Almighty, coupled with humanity, equality and justice." With such a natural, stable, and solid foundation, it shadowed forth the noblest effort of human wisdom.

It was under the foregoing principles that the war of the Revolution was commenced, and so triumphantly brought to its close. It was the departure from those principles, when the organic law of the general government was formed, that induced the great and good Lafayette to remark, "That he would never have drawn his sword in the cause of America if he had thought that thereby he was founding a land of slavery."

Among the enemies of slavery could be counted Washington, Jefferson, Adams, Franklin, Sherman, Livingston, Patrick Henry, Madison, Hancock, Morris, St. Clair, the Randolphs— John and Thomas. Add to the above the rest of the signers of the Declaration, backed up by the great document itself.

We defy and challenge the world to show one single patriot of the Revolution who was in favor of Slavery, or advocated its extension. Some desired its gradual extinction, but not one can be named who spoke in favor of its remaining as a permanent Institution. Well may the poet exclaim:

> "The tender ties of parent, husband, friend,
> All bonds of nature, all in slavery end.
> All other sorrows virtue may endure,
> And find submission more than half a cure,
> But slavery, virtue dreads it as her grave.
> Patience is meanness in a slave.
> Now is the dawning of a better day.
> Come, snap the chain the moment when you may.
> Nature imprints upon whate'er we see,
> That has a heart and life in it, be free.".

WHAT SLAVERY DID FOR THE CONSTITUTION.

The War of the Revolution having been brought to a successful termination, the Colonies began to feel the need of "a more perfect union." Surrounded as they were by savage tribes, self-defence and the general welfare demanded something more for their protection. Thus, in 1787, a Convention assembled in Philadelphia and laid the foundations of our National Government. Notwithstanding the Revolution had been fought and won on the doctrine of equal rights, yet, when the colonies formed a national compact, they set aside the principles on which their liberties had been gained.

The 3d clause of Section 2d, article 1st, relating to representatives and taxes. Capital in general is subject to taxation; but capital invested in slaves is, in addition, allowed representation. "The number of representatives shall not exceed one for every thirty thousand." This excludes Indians not taxed, but negro slaves are counted as *three* to *five*. The practical operation of this clause in the Constitution is, that ten white men owning 50,000 slaves would be allowed one Representative in the lower branch of Congress; while ten who had invested a similar amount of capital, or ten times the amount in *lands* or *merchandise* would have nothing to say except one vote each. They would just lack 29,990 more white persons to be entitled to a representative. Their capital invested in real estate and merchandise might be taxed, but to be represented also, they would have to invest it in *negro slaves*.

In a speech delivered in the Tremont Temple, Boston, Mass., by Robert Toombs of Georgia, Jan. 24th, 1856, he said of the above clause: "This provision strengthens slavery by giving the existing slave holding states many more representatives in Congress than they would have if slaves were considered only as property. Twenty Representatives in Congress hold their seats to-day by virtue of this clause."

Section IX, article 1st, as it reads in the Constitution: "The migration or importation of such persons as any of the

States now existing shall think proper to admit, shall not be prohibited by the Congress prior to the year one thousand eight hundred and eight, but a tax or duty may be imposed on such importation, not exceeding ten dollars for each person."

This section recognized the slave trade for a period of twenty years, or until 1808. Mr. Martin, of Maryland, one of the delegates, proposed to amend that clause, so as to prohibit the slave trade. For, said he, it is inconsistent with the principles of the Revolution. But Mr. Rutledge, of South Carolina, immediately jumped to his feet and remarked, that the true question was, whether the Southern States shall or shall not be parties to the Union. Pinkney, of the same State, remarked that South Carolina would never accept the Constitution if it prohibited the slave trade. After which Mr. Rutledge remarked, if the convention think that North Carolina, South Carolina and Georgia will ever agree to be parties, unless their right to import slaves be untouched, the expectation is vain.

The article was so altered as to allow the importation of slaves until 1800, but this was too short a time. Pinkney, of South Carolina, moved to strike out 1800 and insert 1808, and the motion was carried.

In the original draft of the Declaration of Independence, the slave trade is denounced as piratical warfare. These denunciations were struck out of the Declaration of Independence in compliance to South Carolina and Georgia, who had never attempted to restrain the importation of slaves, and who, on the contrary, wished to continue it.—*Writings of Thos. Jefferson.*

In the South Carolina Convention, Judge Pendleton observed that only three states, Georgia, South Carolina and North Carolina, allowed the importation of negroes. Their reason for so doing was that during the last war they lost vast numbers of them, which loss they wished to supply.

'It was notorious that the postponement of immediate abolition (of the slave trade) was indispensible to secure the adoption of the Constitution. It was a *necessary sacrifice* to the prejudices and interests of a portion of the Southern States.—*3d Story Com. Con.* 1828, 1829.

Mr. Morris, of Pennsylvania, thought it would avoid ambiguity by making the clause read thus : "The importation of slaves into North Carolina, South Carolina, and Georgia shall not be prohibited." *He wished it to be known that that part of the Constitution was a compact* with those States.

The 2d section of article IV. of the Constitution reads thus : " No person held to service or labor in one State under the laws thereof escaping into another shall, in consequence of any law or regulation therein, be discharged from such service or labor, but shall be delivered up on claim of the party to whom such service or labor may be due." This was inserted in the Constitution by the same influence. Butler and Pinkney, of South Carolina, moved to require fugitive slaves and servants to be delivered up like criminals.

Why the word slave was left out of the Constitution. The Northern delegates, owing to their peculiar scruples on the subject of slavery, did not choose to have the word *slave* mentioned.—4 *Ell., Deb.* 175.

Story says that it was agreed that slaves should be represented under the milder appellation of "other persons," not as free persons, *but only in proportion of three-fifths.* The clause was in substance borrowed from that passed by the Continental Congress on the 18th of April, 1783.—*2d Story Com.* 641.

The 15th clause of the 8th *section* of the 1st article of the Constitution, provides for calling forth the militia to execute the laws of the *Union,* suppress *insurrections,* and repel invasions. Gov. Livingston of N. J., from the General Committee, reported this clause as it stands in the Constitution.

Madison, Randolph, and other patriots kept the words *servant* and *slave* from being inserted in that instrument, and substituted in their stead *service* and *person.*

The South has always viewed the above phrases as meaning *slaves* and *slavery* ; while the North has soothed its abolition conscience by boasting that the word slave or slavery is not mentioned in the Constitution. All admit that that instrument did not *create* slavery, for it existed, as an inheritance from Great Britain, long before the Revolution. For over one hundred and fifty years slaves had been held by the Colonists, and if the Constitution had set a limit to the traffic on land, as it did on the sea, we should not have had the present rebellion.

Thus the Union, through the Constitution, was bound up with the sinews and cemented with the blood of the African slave.

The anti-democratic feature of the Federal Constitution was always viewed by the patriots of the Revolution with a jealous eye. James Madison, in a letter to Edmund Randolph, dated New York, April 8th, 1787, remarks: "It is also already seen by many, and must by degrees be seen by all, that unless the Union be organized efficiently on *republican principles*, innovations of a much more objectionable form may be obtruded, or, in the most favorable event, the partition of the empire *into rival and hostile confederacies will ensue.*"

OPINIONS AND POLICY OF THE PRESIDENTS AND CONGRESS FROM 1789 TO 1820.

IN the preceeding pages we have given a concise account of the organization of our Government, with hints on the character, opinions and designs of the managers and actors in the war of Independence. We now purpose to admit what they did, explain what they *should have done, and did not*, and give a truthful account of the consequences that followed.

In governments they denied and repudiated the dogma of ruling by "divine right;" abolished titles of nobility and entailment of estates, evils that originated with despots, and have been continued only for the benefit of the craft. They rejected those assumed rights as antagonistic to Republican Governments. But, while they did this, they left it in the power of the States to retain the most dreadful foe of humanity that had reached their time. Thus the sin of omission became with them downright transgression. The recognition by the Government of the unnatural traffic in human flesh and blood, permitting States to retain laws sustaining the buying and selling, and dooming to perpetual bondage its laboring poor, has proved a national disgrace, and is now the damning scourge that threatens our disolution.

To show the reader the terms by which a slave is held and transferred, we copy, *verbatim*, a Bill of Sale, a South Carolina relic of the rebellion :

SLAVE BILL OF SALE.

"Bill of Sale.

"Know all men by these presents, that I, W. S. Whaley, for and in consideration of the sum of six hundred dollars to me in hand paid, at and before the sealing and delivery of these presents by Wm. M. Murry the acceptor thereof, I do hereby acknowledge to have bargained and sold, and by these presents do bargain and sell, and deliver to the said Wm. M. Murray, a *negro woman, named Harriet, warranted sound*, to have and to hold the said wench Harriet, with her future issue and increase, unto the said Wm. M. Murray, his executors, administrators and assigns, to his and their only purpose, use and behoof, forever ; and I, the said W. S. Whaley, my executors and administrators, the said bargained premises unto the said Wm. M. Murray, his executors and administrators and assigns, from and against all persons shall and will warrant and forever defend by these presents.

"In witness thereof, I have hereunto set my hand and seal, dated at Charleston on the fifth day of March, in the year of our Lord one thousand eight hundred and forty, and in the sixty-fourth year of the Independence of the United States of America.   W. S. WHALEY.   [Seal.]

"Signed, sealed and delivered,
  in the presence of
    "THOMAS S. GADDEN."

This traffic in human flesh is an unpardonable sin against human nature. It has been our great national sin against the Holy Ghost, which can be forgiven neither in this life nor the life that is to come.

Now as governments have no future existence, their sins must be punished here. And as war is one of the most effectual means the Almighty takes to chastise a guilty nation, he has sent it on us in its most malignant form. Not a war against a foreign power, but a war among ourselves—a national suicide. Truly our scourge can only be surpassed by our crimes. No question of sufficient magnitude could have ever been introduced to unite the people of one section against the other in battle array, except this very question of *slavery*.

We shall now give a few thoughts on the policy of the early Fathers; and the reader can rely upon its being a correct history in every particular. When quotations and dates are given, they are from the best authorities and can never be controverted. Of the reasoning and suggestions the world will determine for itself.

GENERAL WASHINGTON'S election, as the first President of the United States, took place in 1789. His re-election in 1793. He gathered around him as his chief advisers, such men as Thomas Jefferson and Edmund Randolph for Cabinet officers, men who were and are well known to have been diametrically opposed to slavery in every form.

John Adams, who was elected in 1793, called to his Cabinet Timothy Pickering, Oliver Wolcott, James McHenry, Joseph Habersham and Charles Lee. All had previously been members of Washington's Cabinet.

Thomas Jefferson, elected Nov. 1801, and re-elected in 1805, chose for his chief Cabinet officer James Madison, and held Joseph Habersham and Benjamin Stoddert. Joseph Habersham had been Post-Master-General under both President Washington and John Adams. He occupied the same position in Jefferson's Cabinet. Benjamin Stoddert had served as Secretary of the Navy under Adams, and was so continued by Jefferson.

James Madison, elected first in 1809, and re-elected in 1813, brought in James Monroe as his chief Cabinet adviser; and when Monroe was elected in 1817, he made John Quincey Adams Secretary of State. During these several Administrations, Congress passed no less than four slave trade acts. The *first* is the act of 1807. The *second* is the act of 1818. The *third* is the act of 1819.

Its first section of the last authorizes the President to employ armed vessels of the United States to enforce the acts of Congress prohibiting the slave trade.

The *fourth* is the act of 1820, making the slave trade piracy. The great blow given to slavery by the Declaration of Independence, caused Massachusetts and Pennsylvania, in 1780, to pass acts for its abolition. New York followed in 1799, by gradual emancipation, to be completed in 1827. New Jersey passed an act in 1784 to gradually emancipate, to be completed in 1820. Rhode Island, in 1784. Connecticut in 1797. New Hampshire abolished slavery in her constitution. Vermont did the same, and was admitted into the Union March 4th, 1791. The North West Territory was made free under the Ordinance of 1787. Maine came into the Union with a free Constitution March 3d, 1820.

Thus for a period of 28 years the General Government was managed by men opposed to slavery. In fact nearly all civilized nations, at that time, were arrayed against it. An act in Great Britain, in 1807, made the slave trade unlawful. Denmark refused to admit African slaves in her Colonies after 1804. The Congress of Vienna, in 1815, pronounced for the abolition of the trade. France abolished it in 1817. So did Spain ; the acts to take effect after 1820. Portugal abolished it in 1818.

HEAR THEIR OPINIONS OF SLAVERY:

In a letter to Robert Morris, dated Mount Vernon, April 12, 1786, Washington says : " I can only say that there is not a man living who wishes more sincerely than I do, to see a plan adopted for the abolition of it. But there is only one proper and effectual mode by which it can be accomplished ; and that is by legislative authority, and this, as far as my suffrage will go, shall never be wanting."

John Adams, one of the Committee who assisted in drawing

up the Declaration of Independence; the man whom Thomas Jefferson called the column of Congress, the pillar of support of the Declaration of Independence, and its ablest advocate and defender, agreed with Washington.

Thomas Jefferson, in a letter to a friend, dated July 31, 1814, remarks: "What an incomprehensible machine is man, who can endure toil, famine, stripes, imprisonment, and death itself, in vindication of his own liberty, and the next moment be deaf to all those motives whose power supported him through his trial, and inflict on his fellow-man a bondage, one hour of which is fraught with more misery than ages of that which he rose in rebellion to oppose."

"We must wait with patience the workings of an overruling Providence, and hope that a way is preparing for the deliverance of these our *brethren*, when the measure of their tears shall be full. When their groans shall have involved heaven itself in darkness, doubtless a God of Justice will awaken to their distress. *Nothing is more certainly written in the book of fate, than that this people shall be free.*"

James Madison, in speaking against the slave trade, said: "It is to be hoped that by expressing a national disapprobation of the trade we may DESTROY it, and save our country from reproaches, and our posterity from the imbecility ever attendant on a country filled with *slaves*." Furthermore, he said, "It is wrong to admit in the Constitution the idea that there can be property in man."

James Monroe, in a speech in the Virginia Convention, said: "We have found that this evil has preyed upon the very vitals of the Union, and has been prejudicial to all the States in which it has existed."

John Jay, the first Chief Justice of the United States, appointed 26th September, 1789, during Washington's Administration, in a letter to the Hon. Elias Boudinot, dated November 17th, 1819, says: "Little can be added to what has been said and written on the subject of slavery. I concur in the opinion that it ought not to be introduced nor permitted in any of the new States, and that it ought to be gradually diminished and finally abolished in all of them."

Our entire volume might be filled up with extracts from these great men's writings and speeches. From 1789 until 1817, a period of twenty-eight years, so distasteful were the slave sentiments of South Carolina statesmen, that through eight successive presidential terms not one of its leading men ever held a seat in the Cabinet of any of the Presidents, save and except Paul Hamilton, Secretary of the Navy under Madison, in 1809 ; and we have the best of evidence that he was a man of liberal views, or he would not have been chosen for one of the Cabinet officers.

SATAN ENTERED PARADISE.

It was on the 8th day of October, 1817, that the Devil entered Paradise. John C. Calhoun, then young, with principles little understood, was chosen by James Monroe as his Secretary of War. Up to this time no question had arisen in the councils of the General Government that threatened any serious disturbance. In 1819 and 1820 Missouri, formed out of the Louisiana purchase, organized with a slave Constitution, and knocked at the door of the Union for admission. This was the first time since the adoption of the Federal Constitution that slavery presented itself in a political aspect. There was a peculiar clause in the Missouri Constitution, not only establishing slavery, but also *forbidding any legislative interference with it.* This was something uncommon in State constitutions, and the doctrine of placing any State institutions above and beyond the reach of legislative authority was received by many as dangerous. Many other objections were made, but finally the controversy settled down on the single question of slavery : *Has a State a right to have slavery if she chooses ?*

In this controversy the excitement ran very high ; sharp words were used by both disputants ; and a division of the Union was threatened on the line of slavery. Finally the exciting controversy was brought to a close by a Compromise, which generally leaves both disputants dissatisfied.

As a sample of how little use a compromise is to either

party, I will relate the following of our worthy President: When the Pacific Railroad question was up before Congress, friends of the New York and Erie Railroad called upon President Lincoln and desired him to use his influence to have Congress adopt the broad guage, so that the Erie Railroad could run their cars through to California. Mr. Lincoln remarked that friends of the Pennsylvania Central Railroad had called on him the week before, requesting his influence in favor of a narrow guage. Says he, "If I was to grant your request they would be dissatisfied, so, gentlemen, I think the best thing I can do is to compromise, making it a little wider than the track of the Central, and not quite so wide as the Erie."

Missouri, with slavery in her Constitution, was admitted; but the opponents of slavery secured, as an offset, the abolition of slavery in all the remaining province of Louisiana north and west of the State of Missouri, and north of the parallel of 36 degrees 30 minutes.

Our treaty, wherein Spain ceded us Florida, and the General Government ceded Texas to Spain, (this territorial trade having taken place in 1819, and taking the two treaties together,) very nearly extinguished slave territory in the United States. Except the diagram marked out for Arkansas, and a few Indian reserves, it cut off all below 36 deg. 30 min., the Missouri Compromise cutting off all that vast expanse of Louisiana north of 36 deg. 30 min. This Treaty gave, first to Spain, second to Mexico, all the slave territory south of the aforesaid line. Coming into the possession of Mexico, it became free. Now add the Ordinance of 1787, ceding the Northwest Territory to the General Government, in all of which slavery and involuntary servitude, except for crime, was forever excluded. By this all the country east of the Mississippi, above the Ohio, and out to the Great Lakes, was made free. And the Missouri Compromise extinguished it north and west of the State of Missouri, and north of the parallel of 36 deg. 30 min., except, as before stated, the diagram of Arkansas and a few Indian reserves.

Thus the reader can see that in 1820 Arkansas and Florida

was the only slave territory belonging to the General Government. The increase of slave States was stopped. And all the vast expanse from the Mississippi river, Lake Michigan, Rocky Mountains, and Oregon, by action of the General Government, was all made free territory, and with the consent and support of Southern men then in Congress, and approved by their constituents at home, who were, almost to a man, then opposed to the further extension of slavery.

The excitement created by the discussion of the Missouri Compromise had been allayed, and all was calm again. Mr. Monroe's term of office was about expiring. Andrew Jackson for President, and John C. Calhoun for Vice President, both slave holders. In opposition to them was Adams for President, and Clay for Vice President. Yet nothing was said in the campaign to arouse the feelings of either section concerning slavery. Jackson, Adams, Clay and Crawford, were all candidates for the Presidency in this campaign of 1825. Jackson received 99 electoral votes; Adams 84; Crawford 41; and Clay 37. Neither of the persons voted for having received a majority of the votes, it devolved upon the House of Representatives to choose from the three highest on the list of those voted for by the electors for President; which three were Andrew Jackson, John Q. Adams, and Wm. Crawford. The votes of thirteen States were given for Adams; the votes of seven States for Jackson; and the votes of four States for Crawford. John Quincey Adams having received a majority of the votes of all the States of the Union was duly elected President of the United States, commencing the 4th of March, 1825. John C. Calhoun, who had run on the ticket with Jackson, received 182 electoral votes, which elected him Vice President.

Mr. Adams was a candidate for re-election in 1829, with Richard Rush, of Pennsylvania, for Vice President, both from the free States. Jackson and Calhoun, both slave holders, were the opposition; yet nothing to arouse the feelings concerning slavery was said by either party. The only question of importance before the voters, was the right of the people to govern themselves. This issue was brought forward on account of the previous election going to the House, and it was openly charged that intrigue and corruption were the leading features of it. Jackson received 178 electoral votes, Adams only 83. Calhoun did not receive as many as Jackson. The falling off was in Georgia, where Mr. Crawford charged home on him his connection with the Aaron Burr Plot.

In the second year of his Vice Presidency, Calhoun and his South Carolina friends, seeing that the action of the Federal Government had been almost unanimous in favor of freedom ; the vast territories, even those that had been acquired from France and Spain, being nearly all made free, they perceived that slavery was hemmed in, and without an outlet it would soon become a burden rather than a profit.

At this time Calhoun's friends started a paper in Washington City, called the United States Telegraph. In this paper he commenced to advocate the State Rights' doctrine. He was very violent for the scheme which he and his slave-holding friends had set on foot, for nothing less than a dissolution of the Union. This was to be accomplished through the doctrine of State Rights. Getting that poison well infused into the Democratic party, backed up by so formidable an element, the State of South Carolina could quietly retire from the Union. To give his ideas more force, Calhoun called a meeting on the evening of the 13th of April. This was Jefferson's birth day. His object was to use that great man's name as god-father for his new political heresy, Jefferson having died on the 4th of July, 1826, and this meeting was in 1830. It was Calhoun's design to put words into Jefferson's mouth that he never uttered. But the news got spread about, and a large gathering was present ; among the rest, President Jackson, who had got an inkling of what was to be. Jackson was called upon to act as President of the meeting. After the 24 regular toasts were delivered, eulogizing the great Jefferson, some one in the assembly called for a volunteer toast from the President. This toast not only proved Jackson's far-seeing statesmanship, but also his devoted patriotism. He rose from his seat, all eyes upon him. In an instant the excitement and bustle of the crowd was hushed into the stillness of death. Without pencil or paper, he did not read anything before prepared, but spoke directly from his heart : " *Our Federal Union. It must be preserved.*" What a storm of applause followed ! Jackson did not say it *ought*, or it *should*, but " *It must be preserved.*"

These were words spoken in the right place and at the right time, and the American citizen does not live, without his mind is rotten with treason, but will say Amen to the sentiment, and tell it to his children and their children's children, to be repeated in all coming time. The general joy and good feeling that had been kindled by the President's happy hit, was interrupted by some friend of Calhoun's, who got on a seat and loudly called for a toast from him. After quiet was restored, Calhoun read the following :

" The Union next to our liberties the most dear. May we all remember that it can only be preserved by respecting the rights of the States, and distributing equally the benefits and burdens of the Union."

The snake now came stealthily from the grass. The Union was put second to our liberties, when it was the only thing that gave us liberty. The rights of the States was then lugged in and placed paramount to the Union, when any man of judgment knows that if the Union was dissolved all the rights remaining to the States would be the right of force, to fight and use each other up—always preparing for war, engaged in war, or suing for peace. This would be the legacy left to the States if the Union was gone.

As we before remarked, Jefferson was to be made godfather to this State Rights heresy. This doctrine of state rights *was, and is yet*, that a State has a right to annul an act of Congress, and resist by force, if need be, its execution. The Virginia Resolutions of '98–99 were so warped and misconstrued by Calhoun, as to favor the above heresy. Mr. Madison, their author, still lived on his farm ; and in letters to Mr. Maguire and Everett, and in his daily intercourse with his fellow citizens, denounced the use that was being made of his resolutions. Mr. Madison's interpretation of their meaning, was that they sustained and advised only constitutional means of redress, while those of Calhoun counseled violence and revolution. Instead, says Madison, of Virginia counseling nullification doctrine, the occasion was viewed as a proper one for exemplifying its devotion to public order, and acquiescence in laws which it deemed unconstitutional, while those laws were not repealed—meaning the *alien and sedition laws*. Calhoun had also dragged the Kentucky Resolutions of '99 into the support of his heresy, claiming Thos. Jefferson as their author. Thus the celebration of his birth-day—although Jefferson was not the author. The resolutions were passed at the same time as those of Virginia, and contemplating the same grievance; yet all the remedies they proposed were pointed out in the Federal Constitution. Both sets of resolutions contemplated only Constitutional remedies. But " nullification," says Madison, " inserts deadly poison in the institution we had labored to construct." Mr. Madison also understood Mr. Jefferson's views, which were likewise being misrepresented.

December, 18, 1831, Madison, in answer to a letter from Mr. Townsend, of South Carolina, remarks : " You ask whether Mr. Jefferson was really the author of the Kentucky resolutions, wherein the word 'nullify' is used, (though not in the sense of South Carolina nullification.) The inference is that he was not. That Mr. Jefferson ever asserted a right of a single State to resist the execution of an act of Congress, is counteracted by nothing known to be said or done by him."

We have now proved that the Virginia Resolutions contemplated only Constitutional means of redress ; also, that those of Kentucky were harmless, being similar to those of Virginia. That James Madison while living repudiated the State Rights heresy, and vindicated the views of Thomas Jefferson, who was then dead, by proving that he held the doctrine that it was not necessary to find a right to coerce in the Federal articles, that being inherent in the very nature of a compact. Having proved by their own testimony that Madison and Jef-

THE REVOLUTION. 21

ferson were both opposed to the *heresy of State Rights*, and that they both claimed for the General Government the right to exercise its authority and power to overcome resistance. Therefore this heresy did not originate with either the author of the Declaration of Independence, or the author of the Constitution of the United States; but with the champion of the slave power, in the person of John C. Calhoun of South Carolinia.

We have now arrived at the point to show the real designs of the nullifiers. Men seldom act without motives, either in an individual capacity or collectively. When the motives are evil, and not likely to be seconded by the public, an ardent desire for success compels the manager or managers to substitute other reasons more in harmony with the feelings of the people whom they aim to deceive.

Although slavery yet lingered, (would to God it had died) no one was bold enough to pray for its recovery, and nearly all would have rejoiced over its death. Southern men had by their votes in Congress shut it out of all the Territories of the United States. Many of the organized states had, and were abolishing it. The General Government was counted as its enemy. The moral and political sentiment of the entire nation was set against it. Against such a heavy sea of public and Legislative opinion, few men in any age would have stepped forward as its champion.

South Carolina, the only State in the Union, except Mississippi, that has more slaves within its borders than free white citizens, furnished the man. He would have come from Mississippi, but for the reason that it had only a surplus of 14,160 slaves, while South Carolina could boast of 110,421 surplus above her white population. Thus the demon, with all the venom of eternal hate, came right from the very throne of the slave power. John C. Calhoun was his name.

After surveying the situation, he began to mature the plan of attack. The will of the people was known to be against the wishes of him and his friends. Nothing was left for him but to throw himself back on the rights of the States. This was admirable, but the object was first to unite the people of South Carolina—second, that being done, all the slave States, like ripe fruit, would fall into the lap of Nullification.

Presuming that a State had an inherent right to *secede*, the next thing was to convince the people of the South that it was their interest to do so. And for this purpose he used the Tariff. The South, being an agricultural region, was easily convinced that a high tariff on foreign imports was injurious to them. He next undertook to explain to the South that these high duties were placed on specific articles, and was done, as special favor, to protect local interests. Thus he said to the people of the South, You are being taxed to support Northern manufacturers. And it was on this popular issue he planted his nullification flag, and gathered around it his friends and dupes. The throne of the slave power, located in South Carolina, was his backer, and the slaveholders throughout the South, who loved slavery better than they did the Union, were his friends, and his dupes were such of the Democrats from the free States as had become alarmed for the safety of the party, and made a close alliance, by agreeing to drop the good old democratic doctrine of the *rights of man, founded in human nature*, and advocated by the apostle of democracy, Thomas Jefferson. These men threw all such rights to the wind, and greedily seized the great instrument of the slave power, *State Rights*. This new bastard democracy meant the right to destroy, peaceably or by force, (when ready,) the Federal Union.

It was thought necessary, in order to get this matter fairly before the nation, to call a Convention. So the 24th day of November, 1832, was set as the time, and Columbia, South Carolina, as the place of meeting.

This was the first open renouncement that had ever been made in any State against the General Government. *And here it is proper to give Calhoun's Vision*, or dream, as he sometimes called it, *and the origin of the spot on the back of his hand:*

It was on the Sabbath, late in the month of October, 1832, Calhoun, after a chat with his friends, retired to his room, resolved to pen the article, or forge the wedge, that was to divide the Union of the States. With treason in his heart, and treachery in his soul, all alone he sat down at his table and commenced to write the Ordinance of *Nullification, or article of dissolution.*

THE VISION.

"While sitting at the table," says Calhoun, "having taken the precaution to lock my door, to prevent the possibility of being annoyed, I thought I heard it softly open. I was then engaged in writing the ordinance to be read at the meeting to be held at Columbia, South Carolina, the next month. My back was towards the door, and being engaged in deep thought, I did not turn round again. A noise struck my ear like the agitation of flowing robes. I looked around, and behold a tall figure stood erect. A death-like fluttering seized my heart; my nerves gave way; my sinews became weak and soft like flesh; my entire frame became unstrung, and trembled, as by instinct, for its own preservation.

" When these awful sensations had passed over me, I rallied as though frightened from the effects of a dream. On opening my eyes, behold an officer, wearing the uniform of the Continental army standing by my table, and, as it were, his eyes fixed upon my manuscript. He gradually raised his eyes from the paper, and looked earnestly into mine. I returned the gaze as well as I could. We remained motionless for thirty seconds, when all at once I felt a chilly sensation of awe pass through me. I spoke, without effort, these words, and I never shall forget them : *It is the features of the immortal Washington; thou hast come from the realms of the dead. For what hast thou come, O, hero of the Revolution?*

" He spoke, in a firm, clear voice : ' John Caldwell Calhoun, desist. South Carolina produced one of the greatest martyrs to liberty, in the person of Hayne, and let it not be written on her history that she also gave birth to the blackest traitor recorded in the annals of time. Look only to an everlasting union of the States. In union there will be peace ; in union there will be prosperity ; in union there will be happiness ;

in *union* there will be *liberty*. Dissolution is political annihilation; it would be *death*.'

"Finishing these remarks, he caught hold of my right hand, and pressed his thumb hard on its back, and remarking, 'Across the articles of dissolution, stretched the skeleton of Hayne, and on the back of your hand will a black spot be visible through the remainder of your life.'"

Calhoun has told this to several of his friends, and always remarking he could not tell whether it was a vision or a dream. In after years, when he would become worked up to great mental excitement in his debates on the right of secession or nullification, he invariably fell to rubbing the black spot on his hand, as though it annoyed him.

If the black spot had appeared on Calhoun's head, instead of his hand, it could easily be accounted for on the ground that he was the first victim to that awful Southern scourge, "*nigger on the brain.*" But we are rather inclined to think that his was only a severe case of a previous malady known as "plantation grip."

Calhoun sent down his ordinance to South Carolina; and on the appointed day, in November, the nullifiers assembled at Columbia, and raised the banner of Secession. The chief grievance set forth was the Tariff, which they alleged was passed to protect manufacturers of the North at the expense of the South. The most remarkable thing they stated in the ordinance was, that they intended to maintain their resolve to withdraw from the Union at any hazard, even to the force of arms. This ordinance was signed by over one hundred of the wealthiest slaveholders in the State of South Carolina, and returned to Calhoun. The Tariff was, as we before stated, only adopted as a means to raise the popular outcry. The Tariff could easily have been changed by changing Congress; therefore there was no cause for secession on that ground.

But we will now prove by incontestable evidence where the real trouble was. About this time Calhoun delivered a speech in the Senate. It was after his Vice Presidency had expired, some time in 1833. He remarked: "The contest will in fact be a contest between power and liberty, and such he considered the present contest between South Carolina and the General Government—a contest in which the weaker section, *with peculiar labor, productions and situation*, has at stake all that is dear to freemen."

One man in the Senate and one in the House had sagacity enough to see the *black man in the fence.*

Daniel Webster, in answer to Calhoun, said: "Sir, the world will scarcely believe that this whole controversy, and all the desperate means which its support requires, has no other foundation than a difference of opinion between a majority of the people of South Carolina on the one side, and a vast majority of the people of the United States on the other. The world will not credit the fact. We who hear and see it can ourselves hardly yet believe it."

John Q. Adams was the member in the House. He said: "In opposion to the compromise of Mr. Clay, no victim is necessary, and yet you propose to bind us hand and foot, to pour out our blood upon the altar, to appease the unnatural discontent of the South—a discontent having deeper root than the Tariff, and will continue when that is forgotten."

If Mr. Adams had put on the mantle of Jeremiah, or Isaiah, he could not have surpassed in prophetic accuracy, or wise discrimination, the above last paragraph.

Mr. Benton says, in his Thirty Years, that the remarks of Calhoun had the appearance of laying an anchor to the windward for a new agitation on a new subject after the Tariff was dead.

President Jackson, in his message to Congress, in 1832-33, puts the hollow cheat of State Rights to rest: "The right of a people of a single State to absolve themselves at will, and without the consent of the other States, from their most solemn obligations, and hazard the liberties and happiness of millions comprising this nation, cannot be acknowledged. Such authority is believed to be wholly repugnant, both to the principles upon which the General Government is constituted, and the objects which it is expressly formed to obtain."

This was a bomb into the camp of the nullifiers, and gave them to understand what they must expect if they still persisted in their treasonable designs. Jackson held to the Union without any *ifs* or *buts*. A favorite remark of his, in conversation with friends, was, that no sectional interest or sectional discontent should ever be allowed to weaken the bonds or break up the Federal Union.

When Calhoun saw these unconditional Union sentiments in Jackson's message, he knew it was a salvo from the peacemaker, shot only across the bow, as a warning to heave to. He knew well that the next discharge would be a broadside that would shiver his piratical craft to atoms. So Captain Calhoun, with his brig South Carolina, and ordinance, rounded to, and continued under the guns of the frigate Constitution, Commodore Andrew Jackson, commander, until Mr. Clay, under the instruction of one of the Commodore's aids, Mr. Clayton, prepared articles of capitulation, which the piratical captain of the South Carolina readily signed, acknowledging the power of the Constitution and nationality of her flag.

As we before mentioned that Calhoun had control of a newspaper published in Washington, here is an extract from a speech delivered by the Hon. Isaac Hill, of New Hampshire, as to its character : " For the last five years it has been laboring to produce a Northern and Southern party, to fan the flame of national prejudice, to open wider the breach, drive harder in the wedge which shall divide the North from the South."

Thus the reader can see that the slave power used every effort to create sectional hate and divide the Union years before either Thompson, Tappan or Garrison came into the field.

Thus the storm originated in the most densely slave populated region of the South. When it reached the Ship of State, the political elements became agitated, darkness covered the southern horizon, while black darkness hovered round the masts of the great ship as it rocked to and fro in the vortex of contending elements. The storm and the sea appeared in desperate conflict which should secure the mighty prize, freighted as it was with the accumulated treasure and precious lives of twenty millions of people, whose hopes of happiness were all concentrated there. Old masters with different hopes, looked on from afar—some hoping that she might sink and be lost in the storm—others shedding tears at her distress, and praying that she might survive, when all at once the elements became calm, the mist disappeared, and revealed to the wondering millions the great ship in all her majestic pride.

Commodore Jackson had subdued the storm, brought order out of confusion, and kindled hopes in the hearts of his countrymen. *Would to God we had them now.*

Thus ended the first effort of the slave power to destroy the Union. It failed, but did not abandon the enterprise; the darker the prospect, the more desperate grew its friends.

AN ATTEMPT TO ASSASSINATE PRESIDENT JACKSON—NEW THREATS OF DISSOLUTION OF THE UNION.

The slave power having been defeated in its first attempt to destroy the Federal Union by the sagacity and courage of Andrew Jackson, withdrew to its den of infamy to devise new and desperate schemes for the future. It feared as well as hated the man who defeated nullification. Calhoun himself became more embittered by reflection, and was frequently heard to say that Jackson was a *tyrant* and *despot,* and better men than he had been hung. In fact, it was no uncommon thing at that time to hear threats against the President's life. The corrupting influence of the moneyed power of the United States Bank joined hands with the slave power, although from very different motives. Both would have been delighted to have heard of Jackson's assassination. But the plot to overthrow republican institutions was far more attrocious. In the presence of a crime of such magnitude all other crimes grow pale. Thus Calhoun had a soul ever ready to betray human nature, with a heart as black as night.

About this time, 30th of January, 1835, while the President with a few members of his Cabinet were in attendance at the funeral of Mr. Waren R. Davis, a Member of Congress from South Carolina, who had just died at Washington, and the funeral ceremonies were being conducted in the Hall of Representatives, where all had congregated, when the ceremonies were over, and the procession had just reached the foot of the steps at the eastern portico, President Jackson, accompanied by Mr. Woodbury, Secretary of the Treasury, and Mr. Dickerson, Secretary of the Navy, on coming out of the door, at that moment a man stepped from the crowd into the open space in front of the President, and at a distance of about eight paces, drew a pistol from beneath his cloak—aiming at the heart of the President, attempted to fire. The cap exploded without igniting the powder in the barrel. He immediately drew from beneath his cloak another, which he had held ready cocked in his left hand, and pointing as before, this cap also exploded without firing the powder in the barrel. At this moment the President rushed at him with uplifted cane ; the traitor shrunk back, and Lieutenant Gedney, of the navy, knocked him down. He was secured by the bystanders and taken before Justice Cranch, who committed him in default of bail. His name proved to be Richard Lawrence, an Englishman by birth, and a house-painter by trade. The pistols were examined and found loaded. Caps were put on them, and both fired without fail, the balls going through inch boards thirty feet distant.

The friends of the President felt it to be a grateful interposition of the Almighty. All looked upon his escape as miraculous, having its origin in the all-wise providence of God. The conduct of the assassin excited and surprised every one. The boldness of the undertaking in broad daylight, and in a public gathering, was all weighed and turned over. The great precaution of the assassin in providing two pistols, fearing one might fail, was argued as evidence of a deep laid plot. Various were the surmises, and finally some one suggested that he must be insane. At this suggestion the Marshal of the District of Columbia called a council of physicians to examine and report. Drs. Caussin and Sewell were the men selected. They made the examination, and concluded not to give any official opinion, but to make their report on questions as they put them, and the answers as he gave them. We give a few of the questions and answers to show the leading features of his mind.

Q. Did any one advise you to shoot General Jackson?

A. I don't like to say.

Q. Have you ever been in Congress, and heard the members making speeches?

A. Yes.

Q. How did you like the speeches of Calhoun, Clay and Webster?

A. I liked them well.

Q. Who would you like to see President?

A. Either Calhoun, Clay or Webster.

Q. Are you friendly to General Jackson?

A. No.

Q. Why not?

A. Because he is a tyrant.

We have given enough of this report to show that this man, whether deranged or not, had strong prejudices against Jackson, and a high opinion of his most bitter enemies; using the word tyrant, a phrase Calhoun was always applying to Jackson. His admiration for Calhoun was supposed by many to be caused by an affinity of interest, or an accidental union of feelings of revenge against a common foe.

Whether this man was induced to attempt to murder the President by listening to his defamer making speeches in the Senate, the greatest of which was Calhoun, or whether he was secretly hired to assassinate him, God alone can determine.

There is no doubt but the death of Jackson would have been received by Calhoun as the tocsin of victory. Add to this his deep and long seated revenge, and you have two very strong motives in a bad man's heart to commit crime. Either Lawrence's intellect was weak, and the storm created by the slave power drove him to attempt the crime, or he was secretly hired by its friends to do it. Either one would fasten the guilt direct or remote on the President's defamers, the principal of which was John C. Calhoun.

We can not dismiss the history of those thrilling events, without giving an extract from Jackson's Farewell Address. As putting down the attempted disolution of the Union was one of the greatest achievements of his Administration, he still saw that a new effort would be made. He says: " What have you to gain by division and dissolution? Delude not yourselves with the belief that a breach once made may be afterwards repaired. If the Union is once severed, the line of separation will grow wider, and the controversies that are now debated and settled in the halls of legislation, will be tried on fields of battle, and determined by the sword. Neither should you deceive yourselves with the hope that the line of separation would be the permanent one, and that nothing but harmony and concord would be found in the new associations formed on the disolution of the Union."

These solemn warnings Jackson left to the nation, just before quitting office and returning to his home to die.

The storm created by the slave power during Jackson's Administration, had become lulled to a calm. Arkansas and Michigan had both been admitted into the Union during his term of office. No slave territory now remained to be formed into slave states except Florida.

Martin Van Buren was inaugurated President on the 4th of March, 1837, and during his term of office nothing very exciting took place concerning slavery. Its friends were evidently recruiting from the Waterloo defeat given them by Jackson, but had not yet determined on the mode of another attack.

In 1839, the Hon. Wm. Slade of Vermont, a member of the Lower House of Congress, presented petitions from his constituents, praying for the abolition of slavery in the District of Columbia. This brought down the ire of several Southern members. Among them, Wise of Virginia, endeavored to prevent Slade from speaking by enforcing parlimentary rules, alleging that he was out of order. Finally, after repeated efforts, a vote was carried to adjourn, sixty-three members voting against it. Here, Mr. Campbell of South Carolina, jumped on a chair, and requested all members from slave holding states to go at once into the District Committee Room, where a meeting was being organized.

Rhett of South Carolina, wrote to the Charleston Mercury, declaring that the Constitution had failed to protect the South in her rights, and advised a dissolution of the Union, and proposed that two persons from each slave state should meet and report on the best means peaceably to dissolve the Union. Although six years had hardly passed away since the nullification defeat, another attempt was now made on a larger scale. *Mr. Patte* of Virginia, became the pacifier in this controversy, and the ire of South Carolina simmered down.

The threatened dissolution of the Union on the line of slavery, made so soon after the defeat of the effort of South Carolina, convinced the thinking men of all parties at the North that nullification was not dead, but sleepeth.

About this time, 1838-9, Mr. Clay made a speech in the Senate against agitating the slavery question. His very speech was agitation, for he could not help but know that any kind of agitation was death to slavery. To speak in its favor is an insult to a savage, and much more to a civilized man, who weighs the actions of men and governments in the scale of justice. To speak against it, drags the hideous outlaw and criminal from his dark abode into the light, who, to be hated, needs only to be seen. It was in that speech Clay made his famous attack on Daniel O'Connell, the Irish liberator. The latter had made some remarks against slavery in the British House of Commons. Mr. Clay, referring to that, remarked: " that he regarded his speech as the ravings of a plunderer of his own country, and the vilifier of a foreign and kindred people."

The political horizon about this time looked rather hazy, although there was no appearance of an immediate storm. The politicians were now beginning to urge the claims of party favorites whom they wish to become presidential candidates. Two financial crises had occurred—one at the commencement, the other at the close of Mr. Van Buren's administration. The banks in the different States had become so crippled by the crisis, that they joined the friends of the United States Bank, and both charged Mr. Van Buren and the Democratic party, with being the authors of all the financial distress.

The Democrats re-nominated Martin Van Buren, with Richard M. Johnston as Vice President, for a second term; while the Whigs re-nominated their old candidates who ran in 1836, William Henry Harrison, of Ohio, and John Tyler, of Virginia, for Vice President. Thus the presidential aspirants for the election of 1840 were brought into the field.

The banks, as before stated, made common cause with the Whig party, and gave their undivided support to secure the election of Harrison and Tyler. Financial ruin was everywhere evident; the political element was charged with national discontent; the people themselves had resolved upon a change. Add to this state of things, the millions of money thrown into the canvass by the discontented banks—it made this the most exciting election ever witnessed. When the campaign fairly opened, the pressure became such that *everything gave way*. The mechanics forsook their workshops, the farmers their plows, to join the electioneering cavalcades that were everywhere to be met moving on to conventions. The thoroughfares were crowded with processions made up from all professions and trades. Mounted on long coupled wagons could be seen on his seat the shoemaker, with his awl and last, at work at his shoe; the tailor down on his bench, plying his needle and thread, with his goose by his side; the sadler at work at his tree; the harness-maker at his trace; the tinsmith at his kettle; and the blacksmith, with his leather apron, tongs and sledge, at work on his anvil; the farmers, not to be outdone, were there with their threshing-floors and help, threshing grain with their old Indian flails; the pioneer and his log hut, with latch-strings outside, and a dog and gun in position within; men in companies of fifty, stripped to the waist, with Indian costumes, having long black hair hanging down to the waist, with quivers, tomahawks, scalping-knives, and bow, all painted and mounted on horseback, going through the various evolutions of Indian warriors advancing to battle; add to this their hideous yell, accompanied with the ring of the anvil and sound of the flail, the sweet music of the band, and still sweeter voice of lovely women, joining in the loud chorus—

> "We'll just take a cup of hard cider,
> And drink to old Tippecanoe."

Never was there such a popular uprising of the people. At Dayton, Ohio, a convention was held one month before the presidential election. The old hero of Tippecanoe was there. The crowd, measured by the acre, by competent engineers, showed one hundred thousand people. A flag-pole and flag on top of a house was the sign for free lunch within. Eight hundred poles of that kind were counted. Men of all ages and conditions in life mingled together as brethren in a common cause. Old grandmothers, with tottering steps, supported by buckeye canes; women with children in their arms; young misses and boys jostling about as the great crowd swayed to and fro.

The election over, Harrison got two hundred and thirty-four electoral votes. Van Buren only sixty.

Thus ended one of the greatest political excitements, terminating peacefully, that ever occurred in any country. The people had triumphed in electing a man of their choice.

The day of political intrigue was now inaugurated. In 1838, during Van Buren's administration, Mr. Preston, of South Carolina, had proposed the annexation of Texas. In his speech on that occasion he remarked: "The treaty, Mr. President, of 1819 was a great oversight on the part of the Southern States. We went into it blindly. I must say the great importance of Florida, to which the public mind was strongly awakened at that time, by peculiar circumstances, led us precipitately into a measure by which we threw away a gem that would have bought ten Floridas."

Another remark in Mr. Preston's speech is worthy of notice. Speaking of the boundary of 1819, he said, "It places a foreign nation on the rear of our Mississippi settlements, and brings it within a stone's throw of the great outlet which discharges the commerce of the Union."

Although Mr. Van Buren and the slave power had made friends, and South Carolina gave him the first electoral vote she had given to any President for twelve years, although there was strong evidence of an understanding, neither Mr. Preston's speech, nor the strong arm of Executive will, could convince the Senate that while Texas was at war with Mexico the proper time for annexation had come. By annexing Texas, we annexed war. And a motion to lay the proposition on the table prevailed by a vote of 24 to 14.

The annexation of Texas now became the great scheme of the slave power. Originating as it did in South Carolina, it came into the national councils with the *smell of treason*. Between 1820 and 1830 nearly three hundred families from the various slave States, mostly from Louisiana, had received permission from Spain, while Spanish authority was still maintained in Mexico, to settle in that fertile region, under the express condition that they should submit to the laws of the country. In the meantime Mexico separated from Spain, and immediately passed laws abolishing slavery in her dominions, and also *prohibiting it in all future time*. This the new settlers in Texas did not relish. Backed up by the slave power of the Southern States, a great number of lawless adventurers from the border slave States went over into Texas, hatched a conspiracy, and organized rebellion against Mexico, and, with a population of less than twenty thousand, declared themselves free. Thus war between Texas and Mexico was commenced.

There was no more slave territory belonging to the United States, except Florida. Mexico had abolished slavery, and passed laws prohibiting it forever. The growth of the slave power demanded more room. The General Government had no territory except that in which slavery was prohibited by positive enactment. By surveying the situation, the slaveholders and nullifiers of South Carolina discovered Texas. Thus Mr. Preston's effort, under Van Buren's Administration, to annex; also, his remarks about a foreign nation being placed in the rear of our Mississippi settlement, had a double meaning: first, they were foreign because it belonged to Mexico; second, it was foreign to the Mississippi settlement because they were slave, and Mexico had declared Texas free.

Thus the greedy slave power, with an appetite not to be appeased, stood watching its chosen victim with the one absorbing thought—*how can I secure it*. It was at this interesting moment that General Harrison came to Washington to assume his duties as Chief Magistrate of the nation. Although born in a slave state, still, like Jefferson, he was opposed to slavery. As soon as he got cleverly warm in his seat, he was visited by J. C. Calhoun of South Carolina, Messrs. Gilmore and Upshur of Virginia, and two others, whose names we have forgotten. These five men had the interest of slavery committed to their care, and the object of their visit to the President was to ascertain his views about annexing Texas. This interview took place in the President's reception room. After passing the usual compliments of the day, Calhoun became the spokesman. He said:

"General, the subject of annexation, I believe, like a motion to adjourn, is always in order. The object of our visit is to ascertain your views concerning the annexation of Texas." To which General Harrison made the following reply: that he had not given the subject that attention it deserved; therefore he could not speak positively as to what policy he would pursue. But he could say this much—if Texas had her independence acknowledgd by Mexico, then, under certain conditions, he would favor annexation.

This was about all that passed on that subject at that interview, and the Southern gentlemen retired. They did not even ask the General what these conditions were. He had said sufficient to satisfy them that he was not the man to carry out their plot, with such men as Webster and Ewing in his Cabinet. Their success was next to impossible. Then for the next best thing. They had staked all their hopes on getting back Texas. The South was perishing for the want of more slave territory, and the defeat of Van Buren by Harrison was now about to prevent their success. They immediately went to see John Tyler at his own home in Virginia, and after explaining every thing to him, he agreed to the great necessity of securing Texas at once, and at all hazards ; but I am powerless, says Tyler. I will leave the management of the matter with you. If I should ever become President I would exert the entire influence of that office to accomplish the object.

This was joyful news. They had found the right man, and only one thing was wanting to get him in the right place. President Harrison was near seventy years old, and a little would suffice to put him aside. He had already lived to a good old age, and received many honors. "He can not, in the course of nature, live but a short time longer. He is surrounded by a bad set of men who will do all they can to defeat our darling annexation scheme. We can not get rid of them without we first get rid of the old man himself. They determined rather than be defeated to murder the President."

On the 17th of March the Chief Magistrate issued a Proclamation convening Congress in extraordinary session for the 31st of May ensuing. He was enjoying his usual good health. "Thus," says Mr. Benton, "President Harrison did not live to meet the Congress which he had thus convoked. Short as the time was that he had fixed for its meeting, his own time on earth was still shorter. In the last days of March he was taken ill. On the 4th day of April he was dead. *There was no failure of health or strength to indicate such an event, or to excite apprehensions that he would not go through his term with the vigor he had commenced it. His attack was sudden and evidently fatal from the commencement."—Benton's Thirty Years*, Vol. XI, 210.

Mr. Benton evidently intended the above remarks to convey to posterity that General Harrison did not die of natural disease—no failure of health or strength existed—but something sudden and fatal. He did not die of Apoplexy; that is a disease. But arsenic would produce a sudden effect, and it would also be fatal from the commencement. This is the chief weapon of the medical assassin. Oxalic acid, prucic acid, or salts of strychnine, would be almost instant death, and would give but little advantage for escape to the murderer. Therefore his was not a case of *acute* poisoning, when death takes place almost instantaneously, but of *chronic*, where the patient dies slowly. He lived about four days after he received the drug.

By referring to the Boston Medical and Surgical Journal, Vol. XXV, 1841, it will be seen, that his case was at first considered complicated Pneumonia, but terminated in gastro intestinal irritation or inflammation, resulting in death in a little over four days from the time of the attack. The circumstances which surrounded the illness of President Harrison were such as to preclude all apprehensions of his physicians of any but natural causes for his sickness; yet let us consider how similar are the symptoms of certain poisons, and the causes of natural disease, or disease from poisons that the best physicians may commit an error in their diagnosis, and not only fail to suspect the existence of poisons, but even prescribe and administer the established remedies, which only augment the difficulty, and, render the action of these poisons certainly fatal, as will be seen by referring to Taylor on Poisons, page 107 : "To the practitioner the diagnosis of a case of poisoning is of great importance, as by mistaking the symptoms produced by a poison for those arising from natural disease, he may omit to employ the remedial measures which have been found efficacious in counteracting its effects, and thus lead to the certain death of a patient."

Again, the same author, on the same page, says that if poisons are taken in large doses, and the person is in health, " the symptoms appear suddenly."

Again, on the same page :

"It is very true that these powerful agents, given at intervals in small doses, do not cause those striking symptoms upon which a practitioner commonly relies as evidence of poisoning. They may then produce disorder, but of so slight a nature as scarcely to excite suspicion. In fact, under these circumstances, the symptoms often so closely resemble those of disease, that an experienced practitioner may be easily mistaken respecting their origin, especially when no circumstances exist to create the least suspicion of criminality on the part of relatives and others around the patient. Arsenic given in small doses, at long intervals, has thus occasioned symptoms resembling those which depend on chronic disease of the stomach. After repeated attacks and recoveries, suspicion may be completely disarmed. Among several cases of this kind which have been referred to me for investigation, was one in which it was alleged that a farmer, in one of the midland counties, had been poisoned two years before by his housekeeper, who was a respectable person, and most attentive to him as a nurse during his illness. He had been attacked at intervals with vomiting and other signs of disorder of the stomach about three months before his death, but recovered under medical treatment. About eight days before his death the symptoms recurred with greater violence than ever, and he sank under them. They were referred to ulceration of the stomach, so closely did they resemble those of disease. As there was no suspicion of poison, the body was not examined; and nothing would have been known respecting the real cause of death, but for a statement made two years afterwards, by the housekeeper, that she had on two occasions administered to her master small doses of arsenic, and the last, probably from its being larger than the first, had occasioned death. In the case of Reg. v. Wooler (Durham Winter Assizes, 1855), it was proved that the deceased had been laboring under symptoms of poisoning by arsenic, for a period of about six weeks before her death. The symptoms showed that she must have received the poison at different periods in small doses. At first they were referred to disease. It was, however, their continuance and their occasional violent recurrence in spite of treatment, that induced a suspicion of poisoning, which was confirmed by a chemical examination of the urine, and subsequently of the body."

From the foregoing quotations it will be seen how natural it was for any physician to have been mistaken in the case; and supposing this to be true, it is very evident that the remedies used in the case, being what Dr. Taylor calls irritants, such as mercury and antimony, and capable of augmenting the difficulty and adding to a condition already established, the cause of which not being suspected could only be followed by the fatal result. On page 109, the same author says: "A diseased state of the body may render a person comparatively unsusceptible of the actions of some poisons, while in other instances it may increase their action and render them fatal in small doses." Again, on the same page, he says: "In certain diseased states of the system, there is an increased susceptibility to the action of poison, or what is termed *intolerance* of certain drugs. Ordinary medicinal doses may in such cases exert a poisonous action. Thus, in persons who have a tendency to apoplexy, a small dose of opium may act more quickly and prove fatal. In one laboring under inflammation of the stomach or bowels, there would be an increased susceptibility of the action of arsenic, or other irritants."

Supposing the fatal agent used to have been arsenic, the use of mercury and antimony in his case certainly would come under the last considerations, "irritants," and cause an increase of the difficulty, and transfer the disease to the stomach and bowels. The whole class of symptoms of active diseases of the stomach and bowels, are closely allied to diseases produced by poisons of this class; and in almost every instance may be mistaken, as quoted above, for *natural* diseases. Such was the fact in the case of General Harrison; and under circumstances that would entirely exempt his physicians from blame or censure for any failure in diagnosis, or the administration of irritants in the treatment; such remedies being according to standard authority in his supposed disease;

while they are never recommended when poisons of the same kind are already in the system. As this case changed so much from the beginning, it is almost certain that the irritants used in the case fully developed the effect of the arsenic which he had taken, and resulted as above stated.

Dr. Taylor, on page 123, says : " The diseases, the symptoms of which resemble those produced by *irritant* poisons, are cholera, gastritis, enteritis, gastro-enteritis, peritonitis, perforation of the stomach or intestines, strangulated hernia, colic, and hæmatemesis." He further adds, page 125 : " *Gastritis, Enteritis, Gastro-enteritis, Peritonitis.*—These diseases do not commonly occur without some obvious cause ; indeed, the two first, in the acute form, must be regarded as the direct results of irritant poisoning. Thus arsenic and other irritants, when they prove fatal, commonly give rise to inflammation of the stomach and bowels. In all cases in which these diseases present themselves, the object of a practitioner is, therefore, to determine the *cause* of the inflammation, whether it be due to natural disease, or the action of an irritant poison."

With these facts, and the quoted authority, can any one doubt that General Harrison was poisoned, and also that his physicians overlooked the true nature of the malady. The attending physicians, Drs. May and Miller, supposed he died of billious pleurisy. His death occurred at half past 12 o'clock at night, Saturday, April 3d, 1841. About noon it was supposed he was getting better, but at 3 o'clock the symptoms became more violent, and at sundown his entire Cabinet Officers were informed that the symptoms were such that it was evident he must die.

All this time John Tyler was absent, at home on his farm in Virginia. Fletcher Webster, Chief Clerk in the State Department, was immediately dispatched to Virginia, to inform Tyler of the event ; and on th 4th, the following official announcement was made :

"CITY OF WASHINGTON, April 4th, 1841.
" An all wise Providence having suddenly removed from

this life, William Henry Harrison, late President of the United States, we have thought it our duty, in the recess of Congress, and in the absence of the Vice President from the seat of Government, to make this afflicting bereavement known to the country, by this declaration under our hands.

"He died at the President's House, in this city, 4th day of April, A. D., 1841, at thirty minutes before 1 o'clock in the morning. The people of the United States, overwhelmed, like ourselves, by an event so *unexpected*, and so melancholy, will derive consolation from knowing that his death was calm and resigned, as his life has been patriotic, useful, and distinguished; and that the last utterance of his lips expressed a fervent desire for the perpetuity of the Constitution and the preservation of its true principles. In death, as well as in life, the happiness of his country was uppermost in his thoughts.

[Signed,] "DANIEL WEBSTER, *Secretary of State.*
"THOMAS EWING, *Secretary of the Treas.*
"JOHN BELL, *Secretary of War.*
"J. J. CRITTENDEN, *Attorney General.*
"JAMES GRANGER, *Post-Master General.*"

On the 9th of April, Tyler issued an address to the people. Among other things, he said: "That for the first time in our history, the person elected to the Vice Presidency of the United States, by the happening of a contingency provided in the Constitution, has had devolved upon him the Presidential office." (He must have felt keenly the sense of guilt that he deserved, and would receive the reproach of his countrymen when he penned the following sentence.) The spirit of faction, which is directly opposed to the spirit of lofty patriotism, may find it the occasion for assaults upon my Administration."

Thomas Benton remarks: "Little did he think when he wrote the above sentence, that within three short months, within less time than a Commercial Bill of Exchange has to run, the great party which had elected him, and the Cabinet Officers should be united in that assault, and should lead the van of public outcry against him."

Betraying and deceiving friends, formed the leading traits of his character. By this course he became extremely unpopular. The number of Cabinet Officers appointed by Presidents holding only one term, run thus: John Adams, 12; John Quincey Adams 7; Van Buren 10; Polk 9; Fillmore 11; Pierce 7; Buchanan 8; John Tyler 21. This outnumbered any of the two-term Presidents. Jackson, during the stormy times of both his Administrations, only had 19. If Tyler had served two terms at the same ratio, he would have had 42.

Thus ends the account of the campaign and election; also of the mysterious and sudden death of President Harrison. We now propose to show more fully the motives that induced his murder, by following up the assassins in the future development of their plot.

We mentioned in the preceding pages that five Southern men had visited the President shortly after he took his seat. We gave the names of three—Calhoun, Gilmore and Upshur —the latter two from Virginia. There were two others in company, but their names have slipped our memory. These gentlemen, after having the conversation with President Harrison, went directly to Richmond, Va., and from there to the Vice President John Tyler's house. They there addressed him, as a *Southern* man, and wanted to get his views on the annexation of Texas. We do not pretend to give the precise words of their two days' entertainment; only to demonstrate to the world that political intrigue and secret assassination were unanimously agreed upon, and afterwards successfully carried out.

Harrison was to be secretly put out of the way, so that John Tyler would become the Constitutional President. To reward those who dyed their hands in his innocent blood, Tyler solemnly agreed to betray the party that elected him, and forever turn his back on its men and its measures; and call, as his Cabinet advisers, the identical men who, by foul murder, had placed him in the Presidential Chair. It was not the

Democratic Party that Tyler had made an alliance with, but it was with the nullifiers and secessionists; men who, in the interests of slavery, had secretly sworn to devote their whole lives to accomplish the destruction of the Federal Union.

The Whig Party very soon discovered that Tyler had turned his back on its policy; and on the 11th day of September, 1841, Senator Dixon of Rhode Island, and Jeremiah Morrow of Ohio, both venerable with age, were appointed Presidents of a meeting held by the Whig Members of Congress. They issued what they termed a manifesto, renouncing said John Tyler. We copy the following:

"That he might be able to divert the policy of his Administration into a channel which should lead to new political combinations, and accomplish results which must overthrow the present division of parties in the country, and finally produce a state of things which those who elected him, at least, never contemplated." Again: "He has *violently* separated himself from those by whose exertions and suffrages he was elected to that office, through which he reached his present exalted situation. The existence of this unnatural relation is as extraordinary as the announcement of it is painful and mortifying."

On the same day of the manifesto, his Cabinet officers, all except Webster, resigned. He waited a short time to endeavor to effect a union of the Whig Party, by which he said he meant the Whig President, Whig Congress, and whig People. But Mr. Webster's stay was short.

This was what Tyler had been wishing for weeks—we mean the breaking up of the Cabinet. It gave him a chance to form a new one. He feels his way carefully, and only at the first selection brings in two of the *secret cabal*, as Henry Clay termed it—Alexander P. Upshur and Thomas W. Gilmore, Virginians. Both of these men had visited him at his house in Virginia, before General Harrison was poisoned. Thus Tyler was fulfilling his part of the contract with fidelity. Webster having remained longer than he was wanted as Secretary of State, had to be removed. Abruptness would have carried suspicion. Therefore, says Mr. Benton, a middle course was adopted, the same which had been practiced with others in 1841—that of compelling a resignation. Mr. Tyler became reserved and indifferent to him. Mr. Gilmore and Mr. Upshur, with whom he had few affinities, took but little pains to conceal their distaste for him. It was evident to him, when the Cabinet met, that he was one too many. Reserve and distrust were visible both in the President and the Virginia part of his Cabinet. Mr. Webster felt it, and mentioned it to some of his friends. They advised him to resign. He did so, and the resignation was accepted with alacrity, which showed it was waited for. Mr. Upshur took his place, and quickly the Texas negotiation became official, though still private; and in the appointment and immediate opening of Texas negotiation stood confessed the true reason for getting rid of Mr. Webster.—*2d vol. Benton*, 30 *yrs. pp.* 562.

As we before stated, the object of the conspiracy, which terminated in the murder of President Harrison, was to secure the annexation of Texas as an outlet for slavery. The crime they had committed was so horrible, that the revenge of Almighty God soon overtook them. On the 28th of February, 1844, a very large gun on board of the Princeton was to be fired as an experiment. Many persons went on board to witness it, among whom were the two Cabinet officers, Mr. Gilmore and Mr. Upshur. The vessel had proceeded down the Potomac below the Tomb of Washington, and at 4 o'clock in the evening, when returning, it was determined to fire the gun once more. Lieutenant Hunt having charge, the guests were feasting at the table, when the word came that the gun was to be fired again. They all rushed out to see. President Tyler also being on board, was called back by some one, while his Cabinet favorites walked, as it were, right into the jaws of death. The great gun exploded, killing only five persons out of the great number. Among the five were Gilmore and Upshur. Tyler was saved from the same fate by being called back to the other end of the vessel. Kennon, Marcey, and Mr. Gardener of New York, (who would have been father-in-law to John Tyler,) were the other three killed.

Sufficient of God's displeasure, one would suppose, had been witnessed to induce this bad man to stop. But no ; the very prince of Nullifiers, the deadly foe of the National Government and peace of the country—the sworn enemy of Freedom, and champion of Slavery—the secret mover of the attempted assassination of President Jackson, and poisoning of President Harrison—John C. Calhoun, was chosen Secretary of State, and John Y. Mason of Virginia, Secretary of the Navy !

Tyler's Cabinet was now gathered entirely from the slave States, except William Wilkins of Pennsylvania. He had what the South called a *reliable Cabinet ;* one that would go all lengths, and stop at nothing, to execute swiftly the will of the slave power.

The ultimate object of the plot, of which the poisoning of General Harrison only served as a means to carry out, remained yet to be accomplished. The scheme was hatched in South Carolina during Van Buren's term of office ; and was the idea of getting more slave territory, through the annexation of Texas. These bad men now pursued that object with a step as sure as time. A meeting was called in May, 1844, at Ashby, Barnwell district, South Carolina. The following is a part of the fourth resolution passed at that meeting : " That the alternative be presented to the *free* States, either to admit Texas into the Union, or to peaceably and calmly arrange the terms of a dissolution of the Union."

At another meeting, at Beaufort, same State, and about the same time, one of the resolutions was as follows : " If Texas is not annexed, we solemnly announce to the world, that we will dissolve this Union sooner than abandon Texas.

In the Williamsburg district, same State, another meeting was held. One resolution says : " We hold it to be better, and more to the interest of the South and southern portion of this Confederacy, to be out of the Union with Texas, than in it without her."

The reader can see by the foregoing extracts the disposition of the slaveholders of South Carolina. " Texas, or disunion !" was the cry. The slave power had, by the foul deed of murder, got control of the National Government; a slaveholding President; a slaveholding Cabinet, except one. It only remained for South Carolina, by threats of disunion, to control Congress. Thus the bill to annex Texas to the Union, while she was still at war with Mexico, was forced upon Congress by the slave power. The bill passed the House by 23 majority, but would have been defeated in the Senate if it had not been for the treachery of Calhoun and John Tyler. Five votes were secured by fraud.

Thus speaks Mr. Benton, (who was himself in favor of annexation, but not by fraud :) " He, the then Secretary of State, the present Senator from South Carolina, to whom I address myself, did it on Sunday, the second day of March ; that day which preceded the last day of his authority ; and on that day, sacred to peace, the Council sat that acted on the resolution ; and in the darkness of a night howling with storm and battling with the elements, as if heaven frowned on the audacious act, the fatal messenger was sent off who carried the selected resolutions to Texas. The exit of the Secretary from office, and the start of the messenger from Washington should be remembered together."

Texas was admitted, and all the consequences of admission were incurred : *war—the state of war—was established.* With force did Benton remark, " As Helen was the cause of the Trojan, and Antony the cause of the Roman civil war, and Lord North made the war of the Revolution, just so certainly is John C. Calhoun the author of the present war between the United States and Mexico."

What could be expected of an Administration that secured its power by foul treachery and secret murder. Tyler betrays the party who elected him. Having dyed his hands in innocent blood, he could not bear the company of the dead man's friends; even the principles that his victim had labored so many long years to carry out, he threw aside and trampled with disdain under his unholy and blood-stained feet. The annals of the world might be searched in vain for such a villain. The man on whose popularity he had been exalted to high position, he reached up to, and stabbed. Well might Henry Clay say, speaking of Tyler: "That he contemplated the death of General Harrison with mingled emotions of grief, of patriotism, and *gratitude*—above all, of *gratitude!*"

He betrayed his party and country, and at last human nature—by practising a cheat on a mighty nation, bringing on a useless and bloody war, for the sole and only purpose of extending human slavery.

War existed between the United States and Mexico, brought about by the foul administration of John Tyler, in annexing Texas. Henry Clay and Theodore Frelinghuysen, in favor of a protective Tariff, were the Whig candidates; and James K. Polk and George M. Dallas were the Democratic, and successful candidates. They went in favor of the annexation of Texas, and received 170 electoral votes, while Mr. Clay got 105. Eight slave States gave their electoral votes to Polk, and five in favor of Mr. Clay.

James K. Polk, the newly elected President, came to Washington and took his seat on the 4th of March, 1845. The chief business of his administration was to recognize the war, and prosecute it with vigor to a successful termination. Although originating and existing in the preceding administration, it was not declared by act of Congress until the 13th of May, 1846. And it was not until the beginning of February, 1848, that it was brought to a close.

The terms of the treaty of peace, as made by Mr. Trist, the plenipotentiary of the United States, with the Mexican Government, included New Mexico and Upper California, with the Lower Rio Grande, from its mouth to El Paso, taken as the boundary of Texas. *These were the acquisitions*, for which the United States agreed to pay to Mexico fifteen millions of dollars, in five instalments, annually after the first. The claims of American citizens against Mexico were to be assumed by the United States, limited to three and a quarter millions of dollars.* Thus terminated the war with Mexico,

---

* The use of this money laid the foundation of the once vast fortune of Corcoran, the well-known banker, traitor, and fugitive.

the great outlay of treasure by the General Government, with the immense loss of life, including many of its best citizens.

Eighteen millions and a quarter was no small sum. Jefferson only paid fifteen millions for Louisiana; and all the foregoing territory could have been acquired from Mexico in treating her respectfully for boundaries for even less than fifteen millions. Add to that the expense of a two year's war, and altogether it amounts to over $200,000,000.

Thus ended the annexation scheme. As it was hatched to get more slave territory, commenced by individual assassination, and ending in war, it was pursued from the beginning with a villainy which crime alone can excite.

We must now take a view of the situation of parties. The slave and free States were now equal in number, and it was impossible to get one lone State admitted, as that would give a majority to one or other of the parties; but by coupling two together, which had previously been done with *Arkansas* and *Michigan*, when one was *slave* and the other *free*, they went in with a "rush." This worked so well before, that it was thought that, like bears in couples agree, Florida and Iowa would make a good pair, since they represented the two great principles of state. If they had been both black, or unfortunately both white, all would have been in vain. But when there was one of each color, they were admitted out of kindness, as lovers together. By this double process it kept the slave and free States always equal in number: but the annexation of Texas had brought in a large amount of new territory. The slave power now began to get uneasy, fearing, legislatively, that it would not be able to run slavery into it. It was *power* that was needed. Like the bachelor who married a widow who had already buried five husbands, when they were about to retire to bed the first night, Mr. Shuttlecock (for that was his name) remarked, "My dear, I have always made it a rule in life, just before retiring to bed, to return thanks to the Giver of all good." " Oh! how delighted I am," says his new wife, "it puts me so much in mind of my first love; Mr. Rogers, my first husband, always did this." Both kneeling by the bedside, Mr. Shuttlecock commenced, "O, Lord, I adore thee to-night in a new capacity; I need now thine assistance more than ever before; *please guide and direct—*" "Stop, stop! my dear," cries his experienced bride, tapping him on the shoulder, "*I can do that;* pray for strength; *strength* is what you need most." It was strength, although of a different kind, that the slave power wanted.

The question with Calhoun was, where to get power to put slavery into the new territories. It was claimed that they were free under Mexico, and came into the Federal Government free. But Calhoun, needing strength, claimed that the American Constitution overrode and annulled all laws of Mexico inconsistent with it. "Grant that," said his opponents, "but where is the authority in the Federal Constitution to carry slavery anywhere?"

Mr. Wilmot, of Pennsylvania, now stepped in and introduced what has since gone by the name of the Wilmot Proviso: "*That no part of the territory to be acquired should be open to the introduction of slavery.*"

Thus commenced the agitation, on the power of Congress to legislate about slavery. It was claimed that slavery had rights above Congress, and above the Federal Constitution also. The excitement on this vexed question began to spread, and the slave power again began to rally its forces. The term of President Polk was about drawing to a close, and it was doubtful whether slavery could be carried into New Mexico or California. The Southern members began to hold nightly meetings in Washington, the result of which was a kind of Southern declaration of independence, setting forth that "Their grievances were greater against the United States Government than our ancestors' were against Great Britain." It was not only claimed, in this new declaration of independence, that slavery was to be prohibited in part of the newly acquired territory, but it was boldly set forth that the General Government was going to abolish slavery in all the

States, and bring on a conflict between the blacks and whites of the South, which might result in the whites becoming slaves.

This declaration was signed by forty Southern members of Congress; and, to cap the climax, Mississippi and South Carolina (the only two States that have more slaves than white inhabitants) passed acts in their General Assemblies calling for a Southern Convention to arrange a new government, to be called the *United States South*.

The presidential election now began to take up the attention of all. The Democratic party had nominated, at Baltimore, Lewis Cass, of Michigan, for President, and Wm. O. Butler, of Kentucky, as Vice President. This was in May, 1848. Yancey, of Alabama, endeavored to introduce into the Democratic creed: " That the doctrine of non-intervention with the rights of property of any portion of this Confederation, be it in States or Territories, by any others than the parties interested in them, is the true republican doctrine recognized by this party. Rejected; 246 against, 36 for. This makes Yancey the real author of the doctrine of squatter sovereignty.

In June the Whig Convention met in Philadelphia, and nominated Zachary Taylor, of Louisiana, for President, and Millard Fillmore, of New York, for Vice President. Taylor had the military prestige of Buena Vista, Monterey, Palo Alto and Resaca de la Palma, which proved too heavy metal for the Democratic candidate.

Martin Van Buren, who had been called *the* Northern man with Southern principles, now accepted the nomination of a third party as a candidate for the Presidency, with Charles Francis Adams as Vice President. The principles of this party were, that the General Government should abolish slavery where it had the power, prohibit its extension, and let it alone in the States where it existed; thus the term *Free Soilers*. The election over, it soon became known that Taylor had carried seven free and eight slave States—163 electoral votes. Cass carried eight free and seven slave States —127 electoral votes. Van Buren and his party got none.

TRAITORS IN CONGRESS.

President Polk's administration, ended with a new threat to dissolve the Union, the old Bug-a-boo of the slave power. After getting Texas, they now wished to dissolve. Polk, like Jackson, loved the Union, and never countenanced anything in his administration that threatened its overthrow. He was exemplary in private life, and in public, only aimed at the good of his country.

At every Presidential election the contest with the slave power became more bitter. Like the miser, its greed increased with its gain; getting much, it demanded more. Eight years before, it had dyed its hands in the blood of the lamented Harrison, and saturated its garments on the gory fields of Buena Vista, Palo Alto and Monterey. *Resting* yet *restless* through President Polk's administration, it now re-appears with all its accumulated pomp, and like the Roman oxen, ribboned and garlanded for the sacrifice.

President Taylor surveyed the situation, and suggested proper remedies to defeat the blood-thirsty foe of the Federal Union. About his first official act was to suppress the Cuban invasion, a darling scheme of the slaveholders to secure that Island at the hazard of a war with Spain. After President Taylor had written his first and only annual message, Calhoun, mortified at the defeat of the Cuban expedition, made a visit to the Department of State, and requested the President to say nothing in his forthcoming message about the Union. But this bad man had little influence over old "Rough and Ready," for after his visit the following remarkable passage was added : "But attachment to the Union of the States should be habitually fostered in every American heart. For more than half a century, during which kingdoms and empires have fallen, this Union has stood unshaken. The patriots who formed it have long since descended to the grave, yet still it remains, the proudest monument of their memory, and the object of affection and admiration of every one worthy to bear the American name. In my judgment its dissolution would be the greatest of calamities; and to avert that should be the steady aim of every American. Upon its preservation must depend our own happiness, and that of countless generations to come. Whatever dangers may threaten it, *I shall stand by it*, and maintain it in its integrity to the full extent of the obligations imposed, and power conferred, upon me by the Constitution."

The slave power had now determined to prevent the admission of California into the Union as a State. It had the requisite population, and had formed a Constitution forbidding slavery; and President Taylor, in his message, recommended that it be admitted. Utah and New Mexico he recommended, without mixing the slavery question with their territorial governments, to be left to ripen into States, and then settle that question for themselves in their State Constitutions.

The slave power had put a scheme on foot in Texas, by which that State claimed half of New Mexico, a province settled two hundred years before Texan independence. It wanted to settle this boundary by force of arms from Texas. But here the President was determined that the political and judicial authority of the United States should settle the boundary.

The wrath of the slave holders now increased against him. Having before defeated their fillibustering scheme against Cuba, recommending the admission of California with a Constitution prohibiting slavery, and advising the dropping of the slavery question concerning New Mexico and Utah, and refusing to recognize the forged claims of the Texan slave holders to half of New Mexico; and to the foregoing his pitting himself against Calhoun, in adding to his Message the above extract, after the arch-traitor had requested that all mention of the Union should be excluded from it, the slave power had now sufficient reason to count him as an enemy, and his history gave them to understand that he *never surrendered*. Those having slavery politically committed to their care, had long before sworn that no person should ever occupy the Presidential Chair that opposed their schemes in the interest of slavery. *They resolved to take his life.*

To show the bitterness of the slave power, we make an extract from Calhoun's speech, delivered after his visit to President Taylor, and after the Annual, Message of the latter appeared: "It (the Union) can not then be saved by eulogies on it. However splendid or numerous the cry of Union, Union, the glorious Union, it can no more prevent disunion than the cry of Health, health, glorious health, on the part of the physician, can save a patient from dying, who is lying dangerously ill."

It was generally understood at Washington that the free soil wing of the Whig Party had the ear of President Taylor. and that Millard Fillmore had but little voice or influence. —*See Ormsby's History of the Whig Party, pp. 312.*

This the slave power understood, and they determined to serve him as they had previously served General Harrison; and only awaited a favorable opportunity to carry out their hellish intent. The celebration of the 4th of July was near at hand; and it was resolved to take advantage of that day, and give him the fatal drug. Being well planned, he received it at the right time, and with the same medical accurcy as did Gen. Harrison.

The political magazine was purposely charged with the restless element of slavery. This was done to prepare a way for the President's death, that it might pass unnoticed in the midst of the general explosion. Notwithstanding the threatening of the slave power, the correspondent of the New York Evening Post telegraphed from Washington, July 3d, 1850, that "the President remains firmly determined to defend the possession of the United States Government to that territory at all hazards." But the last charge was placed in the magazine when Ex-Governor Quitman, of Mississippi, telegraphed to Washington, on the same day, (3d) that he was ready, at the head of 10,000 men, to march on Santa Fe, New Mexico." This was all done to force President Taylor to submit to demands of the slave power. *It failed;* but it placed the torch to the fuse, and amid the excitement of the 4th of July, the explosion took place. It accomplished the object —*victory and revenge through the death of the President.*

The New York Post of the 10th, says: "In the contention which has raged at the seat of Government, the stroke of death has fallen upon one to whom his station assigned no small part of the controversy—the Chief Magistrate of the country, Gen. Taylor." He would undoubtedly have checked, by the most effectual means, any effort on the part of Texas to engage in a civil war with the people of New Mexico. The Post further says: "It strikes us that it is by no means a fortunate circumstance for the cause of freedom."

In the enjoyment of the most perfect health, the 4th being on Friday, he was taken sick in the afternoon about 5 o'clock, and on Monday evening at 35 minutes past 10 o'clock, he was dead. He died from the effects of the same kind of drug as was given to President Harrison. The symptoms in both cases were the same—an inward heat and thirst, accompanied by fever. They were both well and hearty at the time the drug was given, and both died in about four days after taking it. Mr. Benton, speaking of the occurrence, says that "he sat out all the speeches, and omitted no attention which he believed the decorum of his station required. The ceremony took place on Friday, and on Tuesday following he was a corpse. *The violent attack commenced soon after his return to the Presidential Mansion.*"—Page 763, Vol. II.

Gen. Taylor's case being considered by his physicians, (a portion of them having likewise attended General Harrison,) called it "billious cholera," in other words, gastro-enteritis. No doubt produced, as Dr. Taylor on poisons, page 123, says, by "instant poisons." The whole of the circumstances in this case prove conclusively that he had been poisoned. He lived, as before stated, about the same length of time from the date of receiving the fatal drug which caused his death, as did General Harrison. The authority I have quoted in Gen. Harrison's case, is applicable in that of Gen. Taylor's. Well may it be supposed that the assassin who had so managed the poison in General Harrison's case, knew well how to apply it to Gen. Taylor with equal success.

As President Harrison had been assassinated in about one month after taking his seat, it was not considered prudent to immediately dispatch President Taylor. Therefore, for the sake of policy, he was borne with for one year and four months. He was in favor of the good old Union, and was in a position to protect it if assailed. They knew he was a soldier that never surrendered. Patriotic, almost to devotion, and too much of a statesman to see his country divided by intrigue, although himself owning slaves, still like Washington he was opposed to slavery extension, and would have rejoiced to have seen some plan devised by which it could be abolished. They slew him on Independence Day, while pouring out his soul in devotion to his country.

"With increased lustre on the march of time,
Forever may his star of glory shine."

Millard Fillmore now became President. This individual has always been in favor of granting everything to slavery. Taylor, while alive, discerning his truckling disposition, gave him the cold shoulder. Thus, when Fillmore came into power, he discharged every Cabinet Officer that had served under President Taylor, and gathered around him new associates— men principally of *the hush-up policy, who wanted peace in their day.*

It was left for Fillmore to sign the act admitting California, President Taylor having been assassinated before the bill passed Congress. After it had passed, ten Southern Senators offered a protest. Of course their protest amounted to a burlesque. The yeas in the Senate was 34; nays, only 18.

William M. Guyn, and John C. Fremont, were now admitted as Senators from the new State, and thus ended the struggle with the slave power for the admission of California.

Calhoun's last speech was devoted chiefly to that subject. It was read by James M. Mason of Virginia, on the 4th of March, 1850. Calhoun was then sick and unable even to read it. This speech surpassed all that he had before delivered in bitterness against the Union. After asserting that all the principal cords that bound it together had been snapped asunder, and nothing now remained to hold it together except force.

The next move to appease the slave power was the passage of the Fugitive Slave Law. The records and acts of the General Government, from its earliest organization, were scrutinized for authority to fall back on as a basis. This was one of the measures of Mr. Clay's Compromise, which had to have a separate hearing, as he was unable to get all included in one bill. The vote on its passage in the Senate was, yeas 27, nays 12. About twenty Senators did not vote either way, and were mostly against its passage.

President Fillmore signed this Fugitive Slave Bill, and has received the censure of a great portion of the Northern people for so doing. Whether he received sufficient intimation, after signing the bill admitting California, to intimidate him, we are not prepared to say. He is yet living, and perhaps can give an answer. One thing is certain, it has served as his political grave. It is not probable that twenty negroes were ever reclaimed under the action of the law. It was got up solely as a gag to the free States. "*That, or break up the Union!*" was the cry.

The time of another presidential election was approaching, and the flames of revolt were bursting out all over the South. In every quarter disunion meetings were being held, and treasonable toasts being drunk. Many and very violent speeches were made in the South Carolina Legislature.

One remarked: "We must secede . . . . If we can get but one State to unite with us, we must act. Once being independent, we would have a strong ally in England; but we must prepare for secession."

Another said, "He hated and detested the Union, and was in favor of cutting the connection." He avowed himself a disunionist—a disunionist *per se*. If he had the power he would crush the Union to-morrow.

In the Nashville Convention, one member remarked: "Secession, united secession of the *slaveholding* States, or a large number of them; nothing else will be wise, nothing else will be practicable. The Rubicon is passed; the Union is already dissolved." Further: "Should we be wise enough to unite, all California, with her exhaustless treasures, would be ours; all New Mexico also."

The following was given as a Fourth of July toast: "The American Eagle :—in the event of a dissolution of the Union, the South claims as her portion the heart of the noble bird; to the Yankees we leave the feathers and carcass."

One toast given at a meeting in Charleston, South Carolina, reads: "*The Union, founded by ignorance, and continued only by knavery.*"

Another Fourth of July toast was: "*The Union,—a splendid failure of the first modern attempt by people of different institutions to live under the same Government.*"

The administration of Millard Fillmore had become very unpopular with those who placed him in power. If Taylor had been permitted to live, and go through his term with the same determination as he commenced, the Whig party would have become strong and popular in the free States. But Fillmore's course resulted in the entire annihilation of the party which elected him.

During the term for which Zachary Taylor was elected, and Millard Fillmore served, three Senators of high influence in their party went to their final account. John C. Calhoun died on the last day of March, 1850. Henry Clay died in June of 1852. Daniel Webster, who was Secretary of State to Fillmore, died in October, 1852. Neither of the above lived to witness another Presidential election. Calhoun lived to hear the efforts of his two powerful opponents, Webster and Clay, in reply to his, read by Mason, on the 4th of March.

The campaign of 1852, wherein Winfield Scott, as President, and Wm. A. Graham, as Vice President, were the candidates, was peculiar. Fillmore, by his *conservatism*, which amounted to *submission*, had completely disgusted the Free-soil element. It was generally understood that Scott and Graham were under the control of the views of this party. The compromise measures brought about by Mr. Clay in the latter part of his life, were approved by both the Whig and Democratic platforms. Many of Scott's friends said they accepted his nomination, but "spit upon the platform." The conservative or submission wing of the party were opposed to what they regarded as sectional issues.

Franklin Pierce for President, and Wm. R. King for Vice President, were the Democratic nominees.

The platforms of the two parties were nearly the same, and the conservative or submissive wing of the Whig party left Scott and Graham to be supported by the Free-soil element, and went over in mass to the support of Pierce and King, the Democratic nominees.

The reasons for nominating Scott were his alledged *availability* and *reliability*. The platform represented all, and yet it poorly represented any of the party ; it embraced too much for some, and too little for others. With the Democrats, their platform was everything—the candidates nothing. Pierce was unknown and untried; like John Tyler he might betray the party, but they "went it blind." Election over, Pierce got 254 electoral votes, carrying twenty-seven States, while Scott got only 42 electoral votes, securing only four States.

The anti-slavery party first appeared with James G. Birney as its presidential candidate in 1840. It polled at this election 7,000 votes. In 1844, under the same leader, it polled 62,140 votes. The abolition of slavery in the District of Columbia and Territories, was the demand of the party in both the above canvasses. In the contest of 1848 the vote of Van Buren and Gerrit Smith together was 296,232, and that of John P. Hale, in 1852, was 157,296. This party did not carry a single State at any of the four presidential elections. Their newspapers and public speakers charged the Democratic and Whig parties with diverting the National Government from the path originally designed by its founders into by-ways and hedges, for the exclusive interest of slavery. They referred to the proviso of Thomas Jefferson to prohibit the existence of slavery, after the year 1800, in all the Territories of the United States, Southern and Northern ; and they also referred to the Congress of 1784, when six States and sixteen delegates voted for that proviso, while only three States and seven delegates voted against it. These charges concerning the Whig and Democratic party were only partially historically correct, but were prophecies of a coming time, true as any ever uttered by Isaiah or Jeremiah, and were exactly and literally fulfilled by the *Man of Sin*, Franklin Pierce, and his unfortunate administration.

USURPING EXCLUSIVE CONTROL OF THE FEDERAL TERRITORY, AND FORCING SLAVERY INTO KANSAS.

The South have always claimed that the Federal Constitution recognized slavery; and that the slaveholders had the undisputed right to remove with their slaves into any of the Territories belonging to the General Government, and it was bound to protect them. The passage of the Missouri Compromise Act, which excluded slavery north of 36 deg. 30 min., they viewed as a concession (unconstitutional) on their part to preserve the peace of the country. Mr. Douglas placed his authority for disturbing that Compromise, on its being superseded by the Compromise of Mr. Clay, in 1850, which reads:

"*Resolved*, That as slavery does not exist by law, and is not likely to be introduced into any territory acquired by the United States from Mexico, it is inexpedient for Congress to provide by law either for its introduction or exclusion from any part of said territory; and that appropriate territorial governments ought to be established by Congress . . . . without the adoption of any restriction or condition on the subject of slavery."

The following is the clause in the Nebraska and Kansas bill, introduced by Mr. Douglas, which repealed the Missouri Compromise: "Which being inconsistent with the principle of non-intervention by Congress with slavery in the States and Territories, as recognized by the legislation of 1850, commonly called the Compromise Measures, is hereby declared inoperative and void; it being the true intent and meaning of this act not to legislate slavery into any territory or State, nor to exclude it therefrom, but to leave the people thereof perfectly free to form and regulate their domestic institutions in their own way, subject only to the Constitution of the United States."

Many Senators spoke against it. On the 3d of March a long debate ensued; Mr. Douglas speaking in favor of the bill until half past three in the morning. Samuel Houston, of Texas, the *only Southern Senator* who opposed its passage, continued speaking until near five o'clock in the morning of the 4th March, 1854, when the bill was pressed to a vote in the Senate and passed—yeas 37, nays 14.

The bill amended, passed the House of Representatives May 22d, 1854—yeas 113, nays 100; only six members from slave States voting against it—Benton, of Missouri, Brigg, Collom, Etheridge and Nathaniel G. Taylor, all of Tennessee, and Millson of Va. The vote on the final passage of the Senate bill, as amended by the House, was—yeas 35, nays 13.

The repeal of the Missouri Compromise was a great triumph of the slave power. It was a virtual denial that Congress had any power over slavery in the Territories, either to legislate it into, or prohibit it from entering therein.

In a speech in the Senate of the United States, in 1853, Atchison, of Missouri, remarked: "I have always been of the opinion that the first great error committed in the political history of this country was the Ordinance of 1787, rendering the Northwestern Territories free territory; the next great error was the adoption of the Missouri Compromise."

Now the Ordinance of 1787 passed Congress July 13, 1787, just two months and four days before the adoption of the Federal Constitution. It was ceding the Territories belonging to several of the States to the General Government. It commences as follows:

"It is hereby ordained and declared by authority (of Congress) that the following articles shall be considered as articles of compact between the original States and the people and States in said territory, and forever remain unaltered, unless by common consent.

"ARTICLE VI.—There shall be neither slavery nor involuntary servitude in said territory otherwise than in the punishment of crimes, whereof the party shall have been duly convicted, provided always, that any person escaping into the same, from whom labor or service is lawfully claimed in any one of the original States, such fugitive may be lawfully reclaimed and conveyed to the person claiming his or her labor or service as aforesaid."

The last part of the above article was dictated by the same interest and influence that two months afterwards engrafted into the Constitution of the United States the last clause of Section 2d, Article 4th.

While this act made free the Northwest Territory, it also established the basis for the Fugitive Slave Act.

Congress then had exercised the power to legislate concerning slavery in the territories; first, the Ordinance of 1787; second, the Missouri Compromise, of 1820.

The slave interest never acquiesced in either of these measures. They claimed that slavery was above *compromise*, *Congress*, and the *Constitution*; no compromise could restrict it; no Congress could prohibit it from extending into the Territories; and the Constitution guarded and recognized it, while the Supreme Court, as property, protected it. This was the sentiment of the slavery propagandists; while those wishing to restrict its extension in later years pointed to 1787 and 1820, as precedents which sustained their position. If Congress could make free the Northwest Territory, and prohibit slavery above 36 deg. 30 min., why could it not prohibit it from entering any Federal Territory?

The controversy on this question was always exciting Congress, and through Congress the country. Mr. Clay designed his Compromise of 1850 to quiet the agitation. Mr. Douglas, in the repeal of the Missouri Compromise, thought, by removing the question from Congress, the people in the territories might peaceably settle it at their own time and in their own way. But in this (though meaning well) they both were mistaken. The old Harlequin, fresh from his conflicts against the Union in Congress, with mischief in his head, honey on his tongue, treason in his heart, and lust in his eye, seeks out Kansas, which had been kept pure by the Missouri Compromise for forty years. After being kicked out of Congress on the 22d of May, 1854, notwithstanding that entire country was north of 36 deg. 30 min., in defiance of his sacred obligations' with the Federal Government in 1820, he now enters that peaceful Territory, with all his accustomed pomp and show of authority, and commits a political rape on its virgin soil.

The slaveholders not only in Missouri, but in other slave States, took Mr. Clay's and Mr. Douglas's view of the subject, and as early as 1851 commenced to emigrate to that region. In 1854, the excitement in Missouri was intense, determined to make Kansas a slave State.

John Scott's affidavit, page 898, Kansas Committee Report, shows that secret societies were then in existence, to force slavery into Kansas. This was a year before any person entered the Territory through the influence of the New England Aid Society. See the affidavit of Matthew R. Walker, page 898; also, that of H. Rolinson, page 900, which prove that no persons were sent out through that association, until the last of March, 1855.

Governor Andrew H. Reeder of Easton, Pa., and other officers appointed by *President Jefferson Davis Pierce* on the 1st of July, arrived in that Territory on the 7th day of October, 1854. Yet, long before this arrival, the slaveholders had everything ready. Secret Societies were every where organized in Missouri and Kansas, under the names of " *Social Bond,*" " *Blue Lodge,*" " *Friends Society,*" and " *Friends of the South.*" These societies were all got up to drive Free State Men out of the Territory, and to make Kansas a slave State. So completely were the pro-slavery agitators organized, that in the month following the Governor's arrival, November 29, 1854, Samuel Woodson, a lawyer of Independence, Missouri, appeared at the territorial polls at Douglas, for the election of a delegate to Congress, with 200 Missourians to vote. Out of 261 votes cast, only 85 were given by actual settlers.

4th District.—Dr. Chapman's Missourians, from Cass and

Jackson Counties, numbering 140 men, camped out all night; they said they came to vote to make Kansas a slave State. Out of 161 votes, only 30 were legal.

5th District.—Sixty-two Missourians went into this district by the Santa Fé road, and out of 82 votes cast, only 20 were given by residents of Kansas. They also said they came to vote Kansas a slave State.

6th District.—Out of 105 votes cast, 80 were from Missouri.

7th District.—Election was held at Frey McGee's, called 110. The number of voters residing in this district did not exceed 40, only 20 of whom voted; yet 604 votes were polled, 584 of which were from Missouri. Here the Missourians voted for absent friends, whom they said instructed them to vote for them, as they could not attend.

11th District.—Polled 255, of which 238 were illegal.

15th District.—Polled 312 votes. The Missourians from Clay, Ray, and Platt Counties, came, they said, to make Kansas a slave State. One hundred and sixty illegal votes were cast in this district. At this election, Nov. 29, 1854, 1,729 illegal votes were cast, to make Kansas a slave State.

The residents of the Territory were completely overawed, and took very little interest in the election. In fact, not more than one-half of them went to the polls. Gen. Whitfield, the candidate of the pro-slavery mob, was elected. He received 2,298 votes. Wakefield received 248, and Flenniken 305. Thus Whitfield secured his election as a delegate to Congress, for the Territory of Kansas.

All this rascality was practised before the New England Aid Society was in existence, it being organized only the 21st of February, 1855.

In January and February Gov. Reeder authorized the enumeration of the entire population to be taken; it showed 5,128 males, 3,383 females, 2,905 voters, 3,469 minors, 7,161 natives of the United States, 408 foreign birth, 151 free negroes, and 192 slaves—making a total of 8,601.

The Governor now issued a proclamation for an election for members of the Legislative Assembly of the Territory, to be held on the 30th of March, 1855. Thirteen Members of the Council and twenty-six Representatives were to be elected. The high-handed rascality previously practised was known to have been sanctioned at Washington, which gave additional license for its repetition at this election on a large scale. From Andrew County, in the north, to Jasper county, in the south, and as far east as Cole County, Missouri, men were organized into parties, and sent into every council district in the Territory, and into every representative district but one, to vote—4,908 thus went to vote at this March election; they went armed and equipped. S. Young and C. F. Jackson had command of a portion; they had guns, rifles, pistols, bowie knives, and two pieces of artillery loaded with musket balls. This party camped near Lawrence, about one thousand strong. In the evening preceding the election these ruffians held a meeting at the camp, and sent about two hundred of their party into adjoining districts to vote. Those remaining to vote at Lawrence had white ribbons in their coats to distinguish them from the settlers—1,034 votes were cast, over 800 of which were illegal. In the eighteen districts the number of votes cast at this (30th of March, 1855) election was 6,307; total legal vote cast, 1,410; illegal vote, 4,908. The free State vote was 791. Hundreds of free State men were driven from the polls, yet the free State party had a majority of 172 above all the legal votes cast in the Territory.

The members thus elected held caucus meetings, during the coming in of the returns, at Westport and Shawnee Mission, and many of them secretly and openly declared that if Governor Reeder did not publicly acknowledge the legality of their election they would take his life.

The Governor says: "I made arrangements to assemble a small number of friends for defence, and on the morning of the 6th of April I proceeded to announce my decision upon the returns. Upon one side of the room were arrayed the members elect, nearly, if not quite, all armed; and on the other side about fourteen of my friends, who, with myself, were also armed."

The bogus Missouri Legislature, that this same force had indirectly brought into existence, met at Pawnee, July 2d, 1855. The Council was composed of 18 members, 15 of whom were from the slave States, 1 from Ohio, 1 from Indiana, and 1 from New York.

The House of Representatives had 35 members, 29 of whom were natives of slave States, 1 of Kansas Territory, 2 of Ohio, 2 of Pennsylvania, 1 of New York, cursing negro-stealers, and swearing that slavery shall be upheld, and that the virgin soil of Kansas shall never be polluted with the foul stain of Free-soil-ism; the Union only when it protects slavery. Every member of the House was pro-slavery except S. D. Hunter, a native of Ohio, and he resigned. Against this worse than rascality, the free States turned their backs.

The house in which they met had neither doors nor windows, and but a temporary floor. While engaged in this highhanded atrocity, that dreadful scourge, the Asiatic cholera, broke out amongst them. To avoid the wrath which high Heaven was pouring on their guilty heads, they fled to Shawnee Mission. Here the Governor refused to recognize them, except by vetoing the tyrannical acts they were passing. Mortified at such proceedings, he came out against them, and was the author of a set of resolutions passed at Big Springs, the first of which was:

"*Resolved*, That we owe no allegiance or obedience to the tyrannical enactments of the spurious Legislature; that their laws have no validity or binding force upon the people of Kansas."

Gov. Reeder arrived in Washington in the beginning of May, 1855. He had previously written several confidential letters to the President, giving a detailed history of events. Pierce expressed himself, at the first interview, as highly pleased and satisfied with the Governor's course, and, says Reeder, "in the most unequivocal language approved and endorsed all I had done."

But Jeff. Davis demanded Reeder's removal. This placed the President in a new position, and he therefore immediately went to work to induce Reeder to resign. "At the next interview he expressed great fear," says Reeder, "for my personal safety if I returned to the Territory, and offered to appoint me Minister to China, alleging that McLane, then Minister, was about to return home." To this new proposition the Governor remarked, that if he could be satisfied that the people of Kansas would be as fully cared for as if he remained in office, and a successor was appointed who would resist the aggressive invasion from Missouri, he was willing to coincide.

Pierce assured him that he would appoint some honorable, upright, Northern man, who was above intimidation and corruption, and one that would faithfully perform his duty. At this interview he requested Pierce to issue a proclamation reciting what had been done in Kansas, and strongly disapproving it, and pledging his administration against foreign interference with Kansas affairs. Pierce now began to talk about Kansas Emigrant Aid Societies, and *Reeder began to suspect*. At the next interview the Governor said to the President : "It is evident that you are about to make concessions in the wrong direction. I have had a great opportunity to ascertain the facts, and I consider this a clear case of aggression on Northern rights, and whatever of concession or compensation is to be made should be to the North, and not to the South ; the interests (continued the Governor) of the Democratic party and the principles of truth and justice loudly require it."

Pierce, fearing to dismiss Reeder, offers a bribe. "If (says the incorruptible Jefferson Davis Pierce) the vacation of your office could be satisfactorily adjusted, all matters could be arranged in such a way as to promote your *personal interests.*"

The Governor considered himself insulted, and refused to reply, and also refused to resign, and left the room. Pierce waited until the last of July and then removed him. Reeder received his notice to quit on the 15th of August, 1855. Thus ended the administration of the first Territorial Governor of Kansas. He was appointed by the administration as a friend

SLAVERY OUTRAGES IN KANSAS.

of slavery. He said himself that he was always in favor of granting the compromises which had satisfied the South, and secured their rights against the clamors of anti-slavery men. —*Page* 943, *Kansas Reports.*

> The animal in Kansas he was unable to tame,
> Although concession to slavery was his political game.
> The abolition clamor he had always despised,
> But his experience as Governor wide opened his eyes.

Wilson Shannon now received the appointment from the President to take the place of Gov. Reeder. Mr. Shannon went out from the bosom of the pro-slavery administration at Washington with decisive instructions. He proceeded to Shawnee Mission, and in a loyal epistle to the President, dated Nov. 28, 1855, calls the pro-slavery agitators the " Law and order party." The Free State Men, he termed violent "Abolitionists." Notwithstanding the Governor well knew that in April of that year Malcomb Clark, a rigid pro-slavery man had commenced a deadly assault on Cole McCrea, at a meeting at Leavenworth. And it was also known to him how Mr. Phillips, a lawyer of the same place, had been violently seized and taken across the river into Missouri, tarred and feathered, and rode on a rail, and his head shaved on one side ; after which they went through the mockery of selling him at auction, compelling a negro to act as auctioneer. He also knew that R. R. Rees, and other members of the bogus Kansas Legislature, publicly encouraged and justified these lawless outrages. He also knew that officers holding high position, such as Judge Lecompt, Associate Judge, S. G. Cato, and J. M. Burnell, Judge Wood, of the Police Court of Douglas County, and S. J. Jones, Sheriff of the same County, with Marshal Donaldson, had organized themselves and friends, to the number of 30, into a Vigilance Committee. He knew that in their official capacity they winked at gambling, for it was a favorite amusement to join Sheriff Jones in a game of poker at 10 cent ante.

About this time, 1855, John Brown, of Harper's Ferry notoriety, emigrated to Kansas, and settled in Osage County. He was an Abolitionist, and soon became the object of the most violent assaults from the Missourians. One of his sons, Frederick,* was met by a party of these invading ruffians, alone in the road, and murdered in cold blood. His body was stripped of its raiment, and his *privates cut off and stuck in his mouth*. John, another son, for being an Abolitionist, was caught, loaded with chains, and driven on foot before the horses of his captors, from Ossawatomie to Tecumseh. The cruelty was such that his reason was destroyed. The house of the old man, as well as that of his son, was set on fire and destroyed. The female portion of his family were grossly insulted, and attempts made to ravish them. Brown was now ordered to leave the Territory in three days, or submit to be hung. The five men who thus warned him, did not survive many hours. The only reply Brown made, was, "*you will not find me here then, gentlemen!*" Before the next sun rose, they were in eternity. If he had not killed them, they certainly would have hung him.

Brown's fame as a warrior now began to spread; and H. Clay Pate, with a party of thirty-three, started from Westport, Missouri, to capture the old man. Brown heard of his coming, and with a party of sixteen men met Pate at Black Jack, near the Santa Fé road. After a short fight, a few being killed, the gallant Pate surrendered. Coleman, the murderer of Dow, was with Pate, but he was well mounted, and, with a Wyandot Indian named Long, made his escape.

At another time Whitfield raised in Jackson county, Missouri, two hundred and twenty men to capture Brown. The old man heard of the move, and gathered up one hundred and sixty men, and took up a position on the Santa Fé road, where he knew Whitfield would have to pass. Fifty of his men had Sharp's rifles, which would kill at half a mile. The rest of his party he had concealed in the timber to make the

---

* Rev. Martin White, Methodist preacher of the South Church, boasted in the bogus Kansas Legislature in 1856, that he killed Fred. Brown, and *thanked God for it.* The last words were applauded by the members.—*Lawrence Herald of Freedom.*

attack on the flank. Colonel Sumner, of Fort Leavenworth, heard of the expected battle, and came with a squad of dragoons, and dispersed both parties. Sumner remarked that it was fortunate for the Missourians that he had arrived, for Brown was so fixed that he would have killed and captured the entire party.

In 1856 John Reid, a lawyer of Jackson county, and member of the Missouri Legislature, raised three hundred men, and two pieces of artillery, and marched on Ossawatomie. Brown this time was taken by surprise; he gathered his forces, and had barely time to get into the timber which lines the Osage river with only thirty men and a limited supply of amunition. The enemy soon came in full view. Brown, although they were ten to one against him, commenced the fight. Reid, not knowing his numbers, and fearing an ambuscade, would not venture into the woods, and his artillery did but little harm, as Brown's men lay flat on their faces, their guns loading at the breech. Sixty-seven of Reid's men were soon killed and wounded; only two of Brown's men were killed. He retired up the river through the timber and crossed the ford.

Gambling, theft, burglary, forgery, rape and murder, were all encouraged when committed on or against Free State Men or Abolitionists. Speaking of these times, Committee Report, page 65, says: " All the restraints which American citizens are accustomed to pay even to the appearance of law, were thrown off. Homicides became frequent. All the provisions of the Constitution of the United States, securing persons and property, were wholly disregarded. The officers of the law, instead of protecting the people, were engaged in these outrages, and in no instance did we learn that any man was arrested, indicted, or punished for any of these crimes."

Such were the men who represented the Administration of Pierce in Kansas. Reeder having repudiated them, Wilson Shannon was sent out to become their leader and confidential adviser. He assured these bad men that the administration would use, if necessary, all the Federal forces stationed in the districts to make Kansas a slave State. Franklin M. Coleman, a resident of Hickory Point, and native of Brook Co., Virginia, had been to the Shawnee Mission to receive the appointment of Justice of the Peace. Enlivened and encouraged by the remarks of the Governor, he returned to his home, feeling strong in the pro-slavery cause, and on the 27th of November, 1855, shot and killed a peaceable and inoffensive citizen by the name of Dow, a Free State Man, native of Ohio.

Coleman went immediately to the Shawnee Mission, right into the arms of Gov. Shannon, for protection. Not finding Shannon at home, he sought out Sheriff Jones, of Douglas county, who was at or near the Mission at the time. Jones was the Sheriff of the county where the crime was committed. The Sheriff and Coleman went to Lecompton, where, without form of law, without issuing a writ, entered $500 straw bail, and Coleman continued free. As the murder was viewed as political, the free State men threatened vengeance on those who had been instrumental in committing, or justifying the fatal crime. Instead of being punished, Coleman found the officers of the law his justifiers and protectors. This course greatly enraged the free State party. Jacob Branson, a free State resident of Hickory Point, and intimate friend of the murdered man, had, with others, been freely expressing his feelings about this high-handed outrage. One Harrison Buckley, and Josiah Hargis, both of these men were implicated with Coleman in the murder of Dow.

On the 26th of November a large meeting was held on the identical spot where Dow was killed. At this meeting resolutions were passed, one of which reads :

"*Whereas*, Charles W. Dow, a citizen of this place, was murdered on Wednesday afternoon last; and whereas evidence, by admission and otherwise, fastens the guilt of said murder on one F. M. Coleman ; and whereas facts indicate that other parties, namely, Buckley, Hargis, Wagner, Reynolds and Moody, and others were implicated in said murder; and whereas facts further indicate that said individuals and parties are combining for the purpose of harassing and murdering unoffending citizens; and whereas we are now destitute of law, even for the punishment of crime, in this Territory:

"*Resolved*, That a Vigilance Committee of twenty-five be appointed, whose duty it shall be to bring the above-named individuals, as well as those connected with them in this affair, to justice."

It was at this time, when the public pulse had been greatly excited by the murder and outrage, on the very same evening of the meeting, that pro-slavery Sheriff Jones, with a posse of twenty-five ruffians, armed with a peace warrant, which had been procured for the purpose from a pro-slavery Justice, by Harrison Buckley, entered said Branson's house, breaking in the door, at the dead of night, and with deadly weapons in their hands presented and aimed at his head, commanded him to put on his clothes, or they would blow out his brains. Branson being a highly respectable citizen, with whom Mr. Dow, the murdered man, before his death had boarded, his friends met the Sheriff and his party at Bolton's Bridge. Jones, in the meantime, had told Branson that he heard there were one hundred men at his house, but was sorry when he found it untrue, for it cheated him out of his expected sport. Just when this conversation was going on, a party of about forty formed in a line across the road. Jones and his party halted and cried out, "What's up?" "That's just what we want to know; *what's up?*" was the reply. Branson said they had got him a prisoner. Some one in the rescuing party told him to come over to their side; he did so, dismounted the mule, and drove it back to Jones. Jones and his party were then permitted to go about their business. Two of the men who were implicated in Dow's murder were with Jones as aids, and it was believed that Coleman was with him also. This was the alleged cause for *Gov. Shannon's Wakarusa war.*

Sheriff Jones, immediately on his return, sent Hargis with a note to Governor Shannon, informing him of what had occurred, winding up with this: "You may consider an open rebellion as having already commenced, and *I call upon you for three thousand men* to carry out the laws."

[Signed]   SAMUEL J. JONES,
Sheriff of Douglas County.

To His Excellency
 WILSON SHANNON,
  Governor of Kansas Territory.
Nov. 27, 1855.

Shannon immediately authorized Major General Wm. P. Richardson, of Doniphan County, to collect as large a force as he could in his division, and bring them with all speed to Lecompton. Six days after this request was made, Richardson was at Lecompton with about 2,000 men. Word was also sent to Gen. Strickler, at Tecumseh, (distant about 12 miles from Lecompton,) to gather immediately as many men as possible, and come in all haste to Lecompton. Strickler brought about 75 men. Official orders were sent to both of these Generals, dated on the same day of Jones' demand, (27th of November.) Copies of these official orders of the Governor were taken by Jones' force, and circulated in that part of Missouri bordering on Kansas. This part of the State has about 50,000 slaves. The story, as told, was that the Territorial law had been set at defiance, and Jones, the Sheriff of Douglas county, a Virginian, and a strong pro-slavery man, had been threatened with death, and no doubt ere this had been murdered by an abolition mob.

The long wished-for opportunity had now arrived (that was an excuse) to enter Kansas and, at the point of the bayonet, drive the hated free State men out of the Territory. Old age and youth began to assemble at the camp at Wakarusa. Shannon said these men came there to fight; they did not want peace; it was war to the knife; they would come, and it was impossible to prevent them. They came to serve under Sheriff Jones, and he readily enrolled them in his posse.

Generals Richardson and Strickler had under their command about 275 men. The forces thus assembled to commence the anticipated sport of murdering free State men and abolitionists, on the 2d of December, 1855, numbered about 1,500 men, 925 of which were from Missouri. Shannon now began to understand and dread the consequences of calling together the pro-slavery mob.

General Eastin, commander of the Northern brigade, Kansas militia, had written to the Governor, dated Leavenworth, Nov. 30, 1855, that the free State men, one thousand strong, were well fortified at Lawrence, with cannon and Sharp's rifles. Eastin suggested in this letter that the Governor call out the United States troops stationed at Leavenworth. The Governor telegraphed (Dec. 1st) from Kansas City to President Pierce, and at the same time sent a message to Col. Sumner, commander of 1st cavalry, U. S. A., at Fort Leavenworth, informing him of what he had done and requesting the Colonel's co-operation. Sumner replied, (Dec. 1st, 1855,) "I do not feel that it would be right in me to act in this important matter until orders are received from the Government."

Shannon now sent a letter to Gen. Richardson, commanding the Territorial militia, informing him that he had also sent Sheriff Jones a letter stating that he was endeavoring to procure the aid of the Federal forces, and requesting that they use every effort to preserve law and order ; also warning Jones that the forces under him were poorly armed, and would be ill prepared to come in contact with the free State party, who were well supplied with Sharp's rifles. Jones informs the Governor by letter, on Dec. 4th, that he has sufficient force to protect him in serving the writ, and thinks he had better not wait for the aid of the Federal forces, but to "pitch in on his own hook." He tells the Governor that the strength of the free State men has been greatly exaggerated ; he has now in his hands warrants for sixteen persons who were with the party that rescued Branson. On this very day, a mob headed by Judge Tompson and Capt. Price, broke open the United States Arsenal at Liberty, Mo., and took three 6-pounders, swords, pistols, rifles and amunition.

Gen. Richardson writes to Gov. Shannon, dated Dec. 3,

that it is essential to the peace of the Territory that the free State men should surrender their Sharp's rifles, and requests the Governor to give him authority to make the demand.

About this time the Governor had received a reply from the President, stating that he would use all the power at his command to preserve order in the Territory, and to enforce execution of the laws. He immediately sent a letter to Col. Sumner; also the telegraph dispatch he had received from President Pierce; on the strength of which Sumner immediately started with his regiment (Dec. 5th) to meet the Governor at the Delaware crossing of the Kansas that evening. But the Governor did not receive Col. Sumner's dispatch until the morning of the 6th.

Messrs. Lawrence and Babcock, citizens of Lawrence, and representatives of the free State men, now waited on the Governor and informed him that an armed mob was surrounding the town, and requested him to use his authority to preserve the peace, and protect the place. The Governor calculated for the Government troops under Sumner to march into the town of Lawrence, and thus protect the place from assault by the pro-slavery mob of fifteen hundred men under Jones, Richardson and Strickler.

In the afternoon of Dec. 5th the Governor left Shawnee Mission. He went by the way of Westport, Missouri, to procure the aid of Col. Boone, a grandson of Daniel Boone. His object was to procure his influence over the pro-slavery men. They started for Lawrence; on the way they were met by a dispatch from Col. Sumner stating that on mature reflection he had concluded not to move until he had received direct orders from the Government. Boone and the Governor hurried on to the pro-slavery camp at Wakarusa, (within six miles of Lawrence.) This was under the command of Gen. Strickler. Gen. Richardson, who commanded another force of the same character at Lecompton, about 18 miles distant, had been requested by the Governor, with other leading pro-slavery men at that place, to meet him at Wakarusa. They arrived, and the Governor appointed 8 o'clock in the evening at his quarters for an interview. About forty of the leading pro-slavery men were there. They were all, except one, determined on the destruction of Lawrence, to which course the Governor was opposed. The conference broke up about midnight, having accomplished nothing. The Governor informed them that he intended on the 7th (to-morrow) to go to Lawrence, and ascertain to what terms the free State party would accede.

The Governor immediately sent an express to Col. Sumner, informing him that "it is hard to restrain the pro-slavery men from making an attack upon Lawrence; *they are beyond my power—at least soon will be.*" Col. Sumner refused, without direct orders from Washington, to participate. The pro-slavery mob did not want the United States troops to interfere, as they felt all-powerful without them. They now became clamorous, and refused to wait longer for diplomacy, threatened to take matters into their own hands and raise the black flag.

The Governor, on the 7th, entered Lawrence, and had an interview with Gen. J. H. Lane and Charles Robinson. The Governor dreading his own men, felt that moments were hours to the citizens of Lawrence. He there stated he was satisfied that he misunderstood its people and the territory, and that they were innocent, and had violated no law. Not one of the persons against whom Jones had writs, were in Lawrence, and the Governor could not persuade the citizens of Lawrence to deliver up their arms to a mob. He gave orders to Gen. Richardson to suppress any unauthorized demonstrations against Lawrence, at every hazard, informing him that the people were willing to make concessions.

A treaty was agreed on and entered into, on December 8th, 1855. The treaty sets forth "*that the rescue of Branson was without the knowledge or consent of the people of Lawrence, and denies all knowledge by the Free State Men of any organization in the Territory to resist the laws;* and requires Gov. Shannon to use his influence to secure the people of Kansas Territory remuneration for damages suffered at the hands of Sheriff

Jones and his posse, and also affirms that Gov. Shannon never called on the people of any other State to aid in executing the laws. [Signed] WILSON SHANNON,
CHARLES ROBINSON,
J. H. LANE.
LAWRENCE, K. T., *Dec. 8th*, 1855.

The Governor, now issued orders. December 8th, to Gen. Richardson and Strickler, and Sheriff Jones, to disband their forces, as matters had been arranged to the satisfaction of all parties. But the Governor was fearful of a refusal so to do, and on the 9th, next day, put the following authority into the hands of the Free State Men:

"*To C. Robinson and J. H. Lane, Commanders of the enrolled Citizens of Lawrence:*—You are hereby *authorized* and *directed* to take such measures, and use the enrolled forces under your command in such manner, for the promotion of the peace and the protection of the people of Lawrence and its vicinity, as in your judgment will best secure that end.

"WILSON SHANNON.
"LAWRENCE, *Dec. 9th*, 1855."

Major Clark, formerly an Arkansas editor, and one Colonel Burns, of Weston, Missouri, and Dr. Johnson, son of the then Governor of Virginia, on the 6th of December, 1855, while Mr. Thomas W. Barber and his brother, and brother-in-law, were peaceably going from Lawrence to their home, about nine miles distant, when about half way, they were met by a party of fifteen pro-slavery ruffians. Burns and Clark were with them, and they trotted off in advance of the crowd, and overtook Mr. Barber and his party, and commenced firing on them with their revolvers. T. W. Barber was killed; his brother's horse was also wounded and died that evening; fortunately he and Mr. Pierson made their escape. The Barbers were from Preble County, Ohio. Mr. Pierson was from Huntingdon County, Indiana.

These men went out from Gen. Richardson's pro-slavery camp at Lecompton in company with Judge Cato, of the Su-

SLAVERY OUTRAGES IN KANSAS.

preme Court, Judge Wood of the Police Court of Douglas County, and others, to see Gov. Shannon at Wakarusa, all armed to the teeth.

Under such high-handed outrages, is it any wonder that Gov. Shannon had become disgusted with the pro-slavery mob, and, like Reeder, determined, if possible, to shake them off? Thus the effort of Jefferson Davis Pierce to drive out the Free State settlers in Kansas, by calling in the pro-slavery border ruffians of Missouri, under the name of Kansas Militia, resulted in failure. Pierce intended Col. Sumner to use the Federal forces against the Free State Men, and in favor of slavery, and expected him to act on telegraphic authority sent to Shannon; but this wise man refused to do so without direct instructions from the War Department, which did not arrive in time.

Pierce's message of the 4th of March, 1850, endorsing all the pro-slavery Kansas outrages, was the most untruthful public document ever issued. Simultaneous with its issue at Washington, the Free State Legislature of Kansas assembled at Topeka. Robinson, as Governor, issued a message reviewing past troubles. Notwithstanding they expected to be arrested for treason, 22 Representatives and 11 Senators were present. Although the free State men at this time controlled four-fifths of the entire population, and the Organic Act provided that the *Legislature shall be chosen from the residents of the Territory, and that those who vote for them shall be actual citizens of the same.*

The people of the Territory had nothing to do with making the laws that Gov. Shannon and the corrupt administration at Washington were endeavoring to force on them. Shannon and Pierce were compelling submission to the tyrannical acts of the pro-slavery legislature, elected by fraudulent votes from Missouri, by threatening to arrest the Governor and members of the Legislature chosen by the *bona fide* settlers according to the *requirement of the Organic Act of the Territory.*

The legislature of Kansas assembled at Topeka on the 8th of March, 1859, and elected A. H. Reeder and James H. Lane

United States Senators. All of these individuals expected to be arrested for treason, but were determined to make no resistence to the Federal officers.

Gov. Shannon at this time was boarding with Clark, the Indian agent, who had murdered Barber, the free State man, on the 6th of December, 1855.

Under Shannon's instructions, United States Marshal Donaldson and Sheriff Jones, with a very large force of border ruffians, accompanied by artillery, made an assault on the town of Lawrence. The United States forces were not permitted to move from their quarters, or take any part in the contest. Marshal Donaldson first entered the place with a posse, and arrested a number of persons for treason, and seized all the arms he could find. The inhabitants made no resistance to the United States officers. He then went through the mockery of disbanding his forces; after which they were immediately led on by Sheriff Jones; artillery was hauled up, and they opened with cannon on the Free State Hotel. This building was burned; also the printing office of the Herald of Freedom, and other dwellings, were entirely destroyed by the torch and cannon in the hands of the pro-slavery mob. The loss of life by the indiscriminate firing of cannon in a populous city must have been frightful. Many of the members of the free State Legislature were arrested; and Gov. Robinson was arrested at Lexington, Missouri, May 21, 1856.

The pro-slavery men now began to distrust Governor Shannon, and a new plan of continuing the strife was resorted to—that of making raids from Missouri, by bands of from 100 to 300 men, under different leaders, for the purpose of murdering and driving out the Free State Men. This was not done as before, under cover, but in defiance of all law. Shannon became unable to control the pro-slavery element, and in the latter part of the summer of 1856 he resigned in disgust. A second failure of the Administration to force slavery into Kansas.

When Shannon resigned, Daniel Woodson, a Virginian, whom

Pierce had appointed Secretary of Kansas, officiated as Governor until the arrival of Geary. The presidential election was near at hand; and, at the solicitation of Buchanan, not only a new Governor, but a change of tactics in Kansas was deemed necessary to assist in the impending presidential struggle. Gen. Sumner, who was supposed to have sympathy for the free State men on account of his northern birth, was dismissed from command by Jeff. Davis, and Persifer F. Smith, a Louisiana slaveholder, appointed to take charge of the department of the West. In Davis's instructions to his new General, he remarks that "*patriotism and humanity alike require that the rebellion shall be promptly crushed.*" Shortly after his arrival in the Territory, Geary, on the 12th of September, 1856, issued a proclamation, which was read aloud at Leavenworth to the assembled crowd by Mr. Adams. This proclamation demanded that all military organizations in the Territory (except the Federal forces) should disband. The change that had been suggested by Buchanan was to sustain the pro-slavery party by acknowledging the validity of the laws passed by the bogus legislature, and sustain the pro-slavery judicials in their crusade against freedom by arresting free State men. To make the matter appear fair, all military organizations had to be disbanded—border ruffians, as well as free State men. This was the scheme hit on by Buchanan—*to disarm the free State men, and render them powerless for defence.*

Atchison, Reid and Titus had a border ruffian force then in Kansas of 2,400 men, with four pieces of artillery. The Missouri Platte Argus at the time said: "*Geary agreed to carry out what the border ruffians wanted if they would disband, and with that understanding they marched out of the Territory.* The record they left behind can only partially be given. They murdered Maj. Hoyt, of Lawrence, by breaking in his skull, and otherwise mutilating the body so as to render recognition almost impossible. One hundred of them ravished a mother and daughter during the absence of the husband and father at Kansas City. About the same time Mr. Hopp, formerly of Rock Island, Ill., while about three miles on his way from Lawrence to Leavenworth, was shot and scalped, and left dead in the road. They broke up the Quaker Mission at the Shawnee Reserve, where the Friends had a school educating a few Indians, plundering the place, and driving off the horses, while the Quakers were forced to flee for their lives. On Washington Creek, about seven miles from Lawrence, they visited the house of Henry Hyatt, a native of Indiana. A young widow, a friend of the family, had accompanied them to their new home; and in the evening of August 20th, while she was passing from an out-house into the dwelling, she was seized by a band of ruffians, who, before she could scream for aid, choked her tongue out of her mouth and tied it with a string behind her and round her neck, telling her if she made the least noise she would instantly be shot. They then tied her hands behind her back, and removed her to a patch of prairie grass, about 400 yards from the house, and after ravishing her in turn kicked her in the sides and abdomen, and left her (as they supposed) to die. On their way out of the Territory these pro-slavery ruffians, in passing the house of Mr. Buffum, who was just then harnessing up his horse, they demanded it. He explained to them that he had an aged father and mother, and a sister and brother that were blind and dumb, all depending on him for support. "You see," said he, "I also am myself a cripple." They immediately ripped out an oath that he was a "damned abolitionist," and shot him through the bowels. They then took his horse, leaving him in such a condition that he died in about one hour. They sacked the town of Franklin, and scalped a man while alive, and exhibited his skinless head to his outraged friends. On the Missouri, above Leavenworth, the settlers at Kickapoo, Atchison and Doniphan, irrespective of party, were plundered of all they possessed; even the under garments of women and the children's clothes, were stripped from their bodies and carried off by the pro-slavery border-ruffian mob. Lecompton and Tecumseh, both strongholds of pro-slavery in Kansas, came in for a share of their lawless depredations.

SLAVERY OUTRAGES IN KANSAS. 81

In the meantime a force was collected at Lexington, on the Missouri river. This is a town in the State of Missouri where emigrants going to Kansas by water have to pass. All steamboats were compelled to stop here and submit to a search. If any free State persons were aboard, they were sent back; if they had arms, they were taken from them. Thus no more free State emigrants were permitted to enter Kansas by the water route. Colonel Richardson, a Missourian, was also dispatched to the Nebraska line, with a force of 400 border ruffians to block up the land road, and prevent any free State settlers entering Kansas by that route. With all these advantages in favor of the pro-slavery party, success appeared inevitable.

This was the situation on the 29th of September, 1856, when Governor Geary brought the Federal dragoons into the field. Clark, the murderer of Barber, (whom Ex-Governor Shannon had boarded with,) Col. Titus, Reid and Atchison were retained by Geary as his aids. Lane, the free State General, made his escape with a small force, with their arms, into Nebraska. Up to October 14, 1856, not one pro-slavery man had been arrested by Geary. All kinds of charges were made and indictments found against free State men, who were arrested by U. S. Marshal Donaldson, (although they never resisted Federal authority,) supported by the Federal army.

Every hope of the free State party appeared, to the outside world, as crushed by the slave power wielding the Federal Government. Geary's rule was such that it compelled free State men to flee from the Territory for their lives. The slave State of Texas had voted $50,000 to assist the border ruffians to make Kansas a slave State, and large sums were sent from other slave States to the leaders of the pro-slavery bands to encourage them to persevere in aiding the Federal Government to murder and drive out of the common territories all the settlers from the free States.

The pro-slavery agitators in Congress were now anxious to lend their aid to the Federal Executive, in the shape of attaching to the army bill, authority to use the Federal army to put down insurrection in Kansas; which meant, to use it to butcher its free State settlers if they did not give their consent that slavery should be supreme in the Federal territories. The army bill passed the House with the above clause attached; 80 Southern Representatives voted for it, and 21 members from the free States—making 101 votes. The Senate refused to pass it with that clause, by a vote of 25 to 7. It was struck out, and sent back to the House, and the bill was then passed with no proviso as to the employing of the army in Kansas.

Some time in October, 1856, a train of emigrants under Mr. Eldridge, 250 in all, were met by Deputy Marshal Preston, with 700 troops and six pieces of artillery. He ordered the emigrants under arrest, and searched their baggage. They were mostly from New York, Ohio, Indiana, Illinois, Wisconsin and Iowa. They were all discharged by Gov. Geary on their arrival in Kansas, and their arms and baggage restored to them.

Gov. Geary had arrived in time to witness Mr. Buffum die. He pledged him that he would bring his murderer to justice. A warrant was placed in the hands of Marshal Donaldson for the arrest of Hays, the murderer. He was arrested and brought before Judge Lecompte, who released him on bail, Sheriff Jones becoming his surety. This aggravated Gov. Geary, and he immediately offered a large reward for his re-arrest. Donaldson refused to act, and swore he would resign. The Governor induced Col. Titus, who was one of his aids, to make the arrest. Titus, the most rabid of all, and the leader of the band of Southern thieves, was about to leave, with his two companies, to join Walker, in Nicaragua, and, for a large consideration from the Governor, he and his men, who had been kept as a kind of body-guard when all other militia was disbanded, made the arrest. Hays was this time brought before Judge Cato, who refused a writ of habeas corpus, and the criminal was sent to jail. This occurred on the 29th of November, and Titus left, with his two companies, on the 1st of December. This act of simple justice on the part of the Governor completely turned the pro-slavery officials of Kansas against him. They sent letters to the heads of department requesting his removal, and a perfect feud was got up between him and Judge Lecompte. This unprincipled judicial knave had just committed twenty free State men for manslaughter, and sent them to prison for five years. Such an act of judicial outrage was never before perpetrated in the whole history of the country. Gov. Geary saw and felt it; his better nature revolted against it, and they joined issue. He removed the Lecompte trials and ordered them before Judge Cato.

On the 6th of January, 1857, several members of the free State Legislature met at Topeka. Sheriff Jones swore out, and Judge Cato issued the warrants, and the new Marshal, who was appointed to fill Donaldson's place, (Pardee,) made the arrests.

The bogus pro-slavery Legislature met at Lecompton on January 15, 1857. Gov. Geary advised the Legislature to repeal some of the obnoxious laws, and let slavery alone until a Constitution was adopted. Not a single officer in the Territory was amenable to the people or to the Governor; they all held their offices by appointment of the bogus Legislature.

On the 17th of February, 1857, a bill was framed and passed by this infamous Legislature to assist Hays, and other pro-slavery murderers to give bail and escape justice. The Governor vetoed it; but the Legislature passed it over his head by only one dissenting vote. After it was passed, Clark, (whom Gov. Shannon, and Sheriff Jones had boarded with,) the murderer of Barber, gave himself up, and entered bail to appear. The Governor had also vetoed the bill providing for a Constitutional Convention, because it did not provide that the Constitution should be submitted to the people. The bogus Legislature passed it over his head. Geary had entirely lost his influence over the Legislature, and the Convention that assembled to form a pro-slavery Constitution looked on him with distrust.

Judge Lecompte wrote a letter to Attorney General Cushing, dated Jan. 9th, 1857, stating that he regarded Geary's advent into Kansas as "a woful curse to the Territory." Also a large party of South Carolinians, who had gone to help make Kansas a slave State, left for home; passing through Washington about the first of the month, they remarked that they were "completely disgusted with Geary and Kansas."

The Legislature appointed one Sherrard to fill the place of Sheriff Jones, resigned. He being an outlaw and a drunkard, the Governor refused to commission him. He secretly waylaid the Governor, and in order to get him into combat, so as to have an excuse to assassinate him, spit in Geary's face.

The Governor exerted himself to get up an indignation meeting at Lecompton. Sherrard attended the meeting, pistol in hand, and after wounding three persons was himself shot dead by a young man attached to the Governor's suit. Geary, hearing that there was a plot to assassinate him, ordered out a regiment of United States infantry stationed in the town, and sent to Tecumseh for the dragoons who were employed there to guard the prisoners, but it was found that all the ferry boats had been set adrift, and there was no way of passing over the troops. He then called out a number of citizens for his defence. The bogus Legislature had justified the act of spitting in his face. The Governor becoming satisfied that his life would be taken if he remained in the Territory, resigned about the middle of March, 1857.

The officers of the United States army under Gen. Smith, when that Louisiana slaveholder found the Governor would not go all lengths to sustain slavery, also turned against him. In his farewell address, the Governor says: "I have been refused a detachment of two companies, with the taunting reply that 'The United States army is not here to protect you.' A band of fifty men have been organized, ever since I entered the Territory, to assassinate me if I did not go entirely in the interest of slavery. My life was constantly in danger. The murders, assassinations and robberies of the pro-slavery border ruffians have never been told."

Thus ended the administration of Gov. Geary in Kansas.

He was selected by Pierce, at Buchanan's solicitation, to go into Kansas to quiet the excitement, in order to assist in the presidential canvass of the fall of that year, 1856. The fraudulent voting, the arming of the border ruffian militia under the form of law, and the raids, in defiance of all law, of from 100 to 300 Missourians into Kansas to murder the free State men, all having failed, Geary went out to disband all the above auxiliaries, and bring the Federal forces into the field, to make a show of a peaceful settlement of the difficulties, in order that Buchanan might not be defeated. The election was carried by the pro-slavery party, under the banner of State Rights, and slavery in the Territories to be rejected or established by the residents themselves without any outside interference. Stripped of all mask, this doctrine is, that a State has power above the General Government; and slavery is above the control of any act that Congress might pass. In this election the democratic party became entirely sectional, and their ticket was elected on a platform that Thomas Jefferson would have spurned, and Andrew Jackson spit upon.

A resolution was passed in the Buchanan Cincinnati Convention, endorsing the Administration of Pierce. This was for the Southern pro-slavery eye. It was excluded from the platform, and few of the Northern Democratic journals ever published it, and no one of them ever endorsed it. So much for the fork-tongued, cheating convention, that nominated Jim Buchanan, a worse traitor than Benedict Arnold. By this double dealing they secured for him 1,800,000 votes. Fremont, his opponent, received 1,275,000. In the free States alone, Fremont exceeded him 130,000. Add Fillmore's, the Know Nothing candidate's vote, 890,000, to Fremont's, and it leaves the old traitor 325,000 votes in the minority.

What Raynor Kenneth, of North Carolina, a Fillmore Native American Orator, thought of Buchanan, may be seen in a speech delivered in Philadelphia, Nov. 1st, 1856. He remarks: "Buchanan is the representative of slavery agitation; he is the representative of discord between sections; he is the man whom the Northern and Southern agitators have agreed to present as their candidate. If he be elected, at the end of four years more, they will spring upon you another question of slavery agitation."

Pierce's sectional pro-slavery administration had made more anti-slavery men than the lecturers and newspapers of that party had done for twenty-five years. Buchanan, as was expected, carried all the slave States; add to them New Jersey, Indiana, Illinois, and his own State, Pennsylvania, which together gave him 174 electoral votes. There being no separate anti-slavery candidate, as heretofore, Fremont carried the great States of New York and Ohio, and nine other free States, making 113 electoral votes in all. Unlucky Fillmore, or the Native American candidate, carried only Maryland. The anti-slavery converts made by Pierce's administration increased from 152,296 in 1852 to 1,275,000 in 1856. The traitor was about sixty-five years old when elected.

Not only did the South claim that the Territories belonging to the Federal Government were all open to the introduction of slavery, but they *desired* the annexation of Cuba; and Pierce, in all haste, set about to procure it, and solicited the aid of James Buchanan, then Minister to England, and J. Y. Mason, then Minister to France, to assist our Spanish Minister, Pierre Soule, to negotiate at Madrid. In a letter to Mr. Soule headed, "Department of State, Washington, August 16th, 1854," Secretary Marcy says: "Sir, I am directed by the President to request that you call a meeting of three ministers, to meet at Paris, to consult on the best measures to adopt in your negotiations at Madrid."

This meeting was held, but not at the place suggested by Pierce, but in *Belgium* and *Prussia*. We make a few extracts from the letter of reply, dated at

"AIX LA CHAPELLE, *October* 18, 1854.

"The undersigned, in compliance with the wish expressed by the President in his several confidential dispatches you have addressed to us respectively to that effect, have met in conference, first at Ostend, in Belgium, on the 9th 10th and

11th instants, and then at Aix la Chapelle, in Prussia, on the days next following up to the 18th of October."

After enumerating the immense advantage that would accrue from annexing, the reply goes on :

"*Indeed, the Union can never enjoy repose or possess reliable security as long as Cuba is not embraced within its boundaries.*"

[$120,000,000 was the price Pierce wanted to pay for Cuba.]

If Spain should refuse to sell the island :

"*Then the question should assume a new shape: Does Cuba in the possession of Spain seriously endanger our internal peace, and the existence of our cherished Union ; if so, every law, human and divine, will justify us in wresting it from Spain if we have the power.*

[Signed]   JAMES BUCHANAN,
J. Y. MASON,
PIERRE SOULE,"

That part of Pierce's administration, to procure more slave territory at the hazard of a war with Spain, was only rendered more odious by its being notoriously known that the administration was secretly encouraging the getting up of hostile expeditions to invade Cuba, and, to blind the public, on the 8th of December, 1855, issued a proclamation to prevent it.

Gen. Wm. Walker, of Scottish descent, but a native of Tennessee, was now struggling to become master of Central America. He had already fought the battles of Rivas, Souci, Virgin Bay, and Granada, but was compelled to fight a second battle at Rivas on the 11th of April, 1856. In this fight he was victorious, but with severe loss. Don Patricio Rivas was Walker's President of Nicaragua. His proclamation, previously issued, had been received with some favor by Guatemala, Honduras, and San Salvador. The object of Walker's first expedition to Sonora, according to his own statement, was to develope the resources of Lower California, and to effect a *perfect social organization* therein ; and to this he said it was necessary to make it independent. In his brief hour of presidential authority, after declaring independence of

Mexico, his second decree was, extending the laws of the *slave State of Louisiana* over the Republic of Sonora. This was his *record* that induced the administration of Pierce to recognize and encourage him in his new field of operations. After Walker's Minister had been recognized at Washington, the administration authorized a meeting to be held, on the 23d of May, 1856, in the city of New York. Lewis Cass wrote a letter to be read at this meeting; he says : " My feelings and sympathies are with you in the demonstration of public satisfaction at the wise and just measure of the administration, by which the existing Government of Nicaragua is recognized, and will be encouraged to go on in its good work." Add to this Marcy's threatening letter about the same time to Louis Molina, Charge d' Affaires of Costa Rica. That Government was hostile to Walker and his adventurers, and Secretary Marcy gives its Minister to understand that such hostility was viewed as indirectly against the United States Government.

The Washington Daily Union, from the 27th of December to the 14th of March, had accounts of six different expeditions on their way to join Walker. Meetings were held in New Orleans, Mobile, Charleston, Nashville, and almost every other Southern town of note, endorsing the action of the administration, and encouraging it and Walker to persevere in the good work in which they were jointly engaged. Colonel Titus, who, with two companies, had been sent by Florida to assist in driving the free State men out of Kansas, was induced by the administration to start with his force to the assistance of Walker, in Nicaragua. He left Kansas on the 1st of December, 1856, at the secret solicitation of the administration to assist the South, under Walker, in acquiring more slave territory in Central America.

This sectional administration of the *Man of Sin* was now coming to a close. In the brief time of four years it had fulfilled every prediction of the anti-slavery men of the North, and completely corrupted the fountains of the democratic element, and used the prestige of that great party to overthrow its long cherished principles established by *Jefferson, Jackson* and *Polk*. His administration was managed exclusively by the disciples of Calhoun; they annulled the doctrine that Congress had power over slavery in the Territories by repealing the Missouri Compromise of 1820, by which they opened all the Federal territory to the introduction of slavery. They sent armed assassins from the slave States into Kansas to force slavery into that Territory, against the expressed will of a great majority of its actual settlers, a detailed account of which we have already given. They were plotting to acquire the island of Cuba, at the hazard of a war with Spain. They allied themselves with and encouraged Walker in his disreputable and subsequent disastrous failure to extend slavery into Central America. They perverted justice, by influencing the Supreme Court to join in their unholy pro-slavery crusade, and compelled Judge Taney to keep *secret* his unrighteous decision in the Dred Scott case until after the presidential election—he holding it in his pocket over six months—that their new candidate (Buchanan) might not be defeated by its promulgation. After the desirable object had been accomplished it was made public, March 6th, 1857, two days after Buchanan's inauguration.

To provide against Buchanan's defeat by Fremont, the administration had arranged, according to a previously required *pledge*, to betray the United States Government into the hands of the ultra pro-slavery men of the Southern States. The proof of this can be found in the Washington correspondence of the New Orleans Delta, dated Sep. 10th, 1856, which says: "If Fremont is elected, Virginia, Georgia and South Carolina will immediately withdraw from the Union, before Fremont can get hold of the army and navy or pursestrings of the Government. Wise, of Virginia, is actively at work, and the South *can rely on President Pierce in the emergency contemplated.*"

Buchanan now began to arrange for the presidential term for which he had been elected. The ultra pro-slavery men of the South determined to control or kill him. They expected he would be the last President that the pro-slavery party could ever elect, and they were determined to have four years exclusive control, so as to disarm the Federal Government. Pierce stood ready, if Fremont had been elected, in 1856, to betray his country. Buchanan *might* be sure, but Breckinridge *they knew* to be safe. Like Butler, Gordon and Leslie, of Wallenstein memory, they resolved to take the life of their leader. Who acted the part of Capt. Devereux, in attempting to assassinate Buchanan, we know not.

THE ATTEMPT TO MURDER PRESIDENT BUCHANAN.

Presidents Harrison and Taylor had been singly assassinated. The first had been dispatched with such perfect success, and a period of ten years having nearly elapsed, and no arrests having been made, it was thought safe to apply the same means to destroy President Taylor. Although the first had twice succeeded without detection, still a repetition for a third time of poisoning a President during the early part of his term of office, and amid high political excitement, it was thought would be surrounded with evidence of foul play, and thus lead to detection.

Therefore, to prevent suspicion and investigation, a change of tactics was determined upon. Instead of the President (as heretofore) being the only victim, it was so arranged that from twenty to fifty persons were to lose their lives, and *among them President Buchanan.* It would thus appear as an accidental occurrence.

Every effort had in each case been made to use the Chief Magistrate exclusively for the *slave interest*, and only when these efforts had failed was murder used to secure victory. The slave interest was led to believe, by Buchanan's political life, and by intimations from the old public functionary himself, that his administration would be rigidly pro-slavery. The Kansas troubles were at their height. Through the repeal of the Missouri Compromise, slavery had a chance in that territory, and Jefferson Davis, and Hunter, of Virginia, and Toombs, of Georgia, with other disciples of Calhoun, were

POISONING OF PRESIDENT BUCHANAN. 91·

determined to rule and direct the incoming administration. Every effort was resorted to for the purpose of compelling Buchanan to make up his Cabinet from the pro-slavery, disunion Southern element. The old gentleman became very stiff in the back after his election, and began to think he was his own master; the country appeared to him to have a Northern as well as a Southern interest, and he refused to be controlled.

He visited Washington in the latter part of February, and put up, as usual, at the National Hotel. On Sunday, the 22d day of February, it became generally known that he had set his face strongly against the Jeff. Davis, pro-slavery rule or ruin party. It was given out that Lewis Cass, of Michigan, and Howell Cobb, of Georgia, were to have the leading positions in his Cabinet.

"He had also promised to settle the question of the freedom of the territories to the satisfaction of the people of the free States."—*New York Eve. Post.*

"The appointment of Cass and Cobb to the two commanding positions in the Cabinet strikes the secessionists between wind and water, and is equivalent to a practical and absolute repudiation of the border-ruffian, Kansas, negro-agitation, disunion policy of Pierce."—*New York Herald, Feb.* 22, 1857.

The *Herald* of the 26th says: "The appointments, by the Jefferson Davis faction, will doubtless be *accepted and treated as a declaration of war, and as a war of extermination* on one side or the other."

On the 22d, Buchanan's determination became known; and on the 23d of February, 1857, (next day,) he was poisoned. The plot was deep, and planned with skill. Mr. Buchanan, as is customary with men in his station, had a table, or chairs, reserved for him and his friends. The President was known to be an inveterate tea-drinker; in fact, Northern people rarely drink anything else in the evening. Southern men mostly prefer coffee. Thus, to make sure of Buchanan, and cause as many deaths in the North as possible, arsenic was sprinkled in the sugar bowls containing the tea or lump sugar, and set on the table where he was to sit. The pulverized sugar used for coffee setting on the table was kept free from the poisonous drug by deep-laid strategy; thus, not a single Southern man was affected. Fifty or sixty persons dined at different intervals at that table that evening; and as near as we can ascertain about thirty-eight died from the effects of the poison.

Mr. Buchanan was poisoned, and with great difficulty preserved his life. His physician treated him understandingly, from instructions given by himself as to the cause of his disease, for he understood well what was the matter. We make the above statement from the highest authority, and as to the material facts we feel confident that the Ex-President, although not our author, will not contradict them.

Shortly after the occurrence, the *Cincinnati Commercial* had an article headed as follows:

"*Poisoning the President.*—Mr. Buchanan, it is well known, has suffered terribly from the epidemic, and is by no means at this time in good health. A gentleman of our acquaintance, passing through Washington a few days since, happened to hear confirmation of the fact from Mr. Buchanan himself." The *Commercial* says, "We take the liberty of quoting the following from a private letter: 'As I was passing a gas light I saw a couple of gentlemen, one of whom, although I had not seen him for sixteen years, I almost knew to be the President. I stepped alongside, and a glance confirmed me; I was not mistaken. The old man totters; his legs are weak. A half stumble drew some remark from his companion which I did not hear. His reply was: '*I am not right; my health is not recovered; adding, in a sort of begging tone, 'but I am getting better.*'"

"*Killing the President.*—When elected President, Mr. Buchanan was in the *highest physical condition*. A few days before the inauguration he visited the Capital, and on returning to Wheatland was slightly affected with an epidemic prevailing at the Capital at the time."—*New York Herald, March 14th,* 1855.

"Since the appearance of the epidemic the tables of the National Hotel have been almost empty. But more remarkable than the appearance of the mysterious epidemic itself, is the supineness of the Washington authorities in regard to it. Have the proprietors of the hotel, or clerks or servants suffered from this disease? If not, in what respect has their *diet* and accommodations differed from those of the guests. There is more in this calamity than meets the eye. It is not a matter to be trifled with."—*New York Post, March* 18, 1857.

Those having a hand in the foul crime, in order to delude investigation, said the disease resulted from the water in the cistern, into which a number of rats that had been poisoned with arsenic had plunged. The Board of Health met on the evening of March 16th. The sewerage of the establishment was pointed to and observed. All the drains, it appears, were south, and southern winds were supposed to have an effect. But how, it may be asked, did a cause which existed for so long a time only begin to produce a fatal effect immediately on the arrival of President Buchanan in Washington? The *South Side Democrat*, Petersburg, Va., says: "Is boasted modern science so completely in the dark that it cannot detect the difference of effect between mephitic air and *arsenic?*"

Symptoms of the attack, and Names of some of the Murdered Dead.—A persistent diarrhea, in some cases accompanied with violent vomiting, and always with a most depressing loss of strength and spirits in the person. Sometimes for one day the patients would be filled with hopes of recovery, then relapse back again into loss of spirits and illness.

Mr. Lenox, of Ohio, died on his way home from Washington. He was a guest at the National at the time of the occurrence.

Mrs. J. L. Adams, of New York city, also died from the effects of this disease. "A post-mortem examination of Mrs. Adams revealed the fact that the stomach had been partly eaten away by *arsenic.*"—*See New York Post, March* 14, 1857.

Mrs. Robert Johnston, of Newark, N. J., after an illness of five weeks, died. Mrs. Johnston, and daughter, and husband had been at the National Hotel at the time. Mr. Johnston and the daughter were also severely afflicted, but recovered.—*Newark Advertiser, April* 16*th*, 1857.

Elliott Eskridge, Mr. Buchanan's nephew, was believed to have died from the same cause.

The following individuals were also poisoned at the time, but recovered: Hon. Robert B. Hall, member of Congress from Massachusetts; Hon. O. B. Matteson, of New York State; Benj. F. Butler, (now Brigadier General,) of Mass.; John Appleton, editor of the *Union*, Washington, D. C.; J. Glancy Jones, of Pennsylvania; Samuel Medary, of Columbus, Ohio; Wilson G. Hunt, G. Gifford, and Marshal Hillyer, all of the city of New York. The latter gentleman's physicians detected *arsenic* in the contents of his stomach.

Intimidated by the attempted assassination, Buchanan became more than ever the tool of the slave power. He now, in conversation with Southern ultras, boastingly remarked, that, "*in the repeal of the Missouri Compromise the South, for the first time in the history of our Government, had obtained its rights.*" So wrote the correspondent of the Huntsville (Ala.) Democrat.

Gov. Geary explained fully to the President the true condition of Kansas, and offered to return, if he would furnish him the military required to protect him against the border ruffians. Clark, Calhoun and Whitfield were now in Washington, demanding Geary's removal. It now became known that Mc Lane, chief clerk of the surveyors office in Kansas, had intercepted, read and destroyed two bushels of letters going from and directed to Gov. Geary. The contents of some of the intercepted letters were communicated to the leaders of the pro-slavery party, and as many of these epistles bitterly denounced them, it was a miracle that he ever came out of the Territory alive.

Buchanan commenced his administration in Kansas affairs as though the entire territories of the United States belonged exclusively to the slave drivers. Lecompte was retained as Judge, and Whitfield, Emery, Woodson and Anson were also kept in office. Thus the judiciary, land officers, public surveyors and marshals were all of the same stripe. Robert J. Walker, formerly of Mississippi, was appointed Governor, and another desperate effort made to force slavery into Kansas. All the power asked for by Geary was readily promised to Walker. Buchanan, through his Secretary, Fred. P. Stanton, of Kentucky, in an address published in the Lecompton Union, the latter part of April, 1857, says that the "*administration has recognized the authority of the territorial Legislature, and the validity of the territorial laws,* (one law of which was that rebellion against territorial law was punishable with death,) *and has especially recognized the act providing for a Constitutional Convention.*"

Gov. Walker arrived in the Territory the last of May. On the 3d of June, in his inaugural, he remarks that "the territorial enactments must be obeyed, and he wishes all parties to take part in the elections, and hopes that the Constitution will be submitted to the people." He was willing to sustain the pro-slavery party in enforcing obedience to the laws passed by the bogus territorial Legislature of 1855. He proclaimed that he would use the United States troops to prevent illegal voting at the polls; but when told that Missourians were coming over to vote, he refused to send troops to the exposed border. He had also procured writs against forty or fifty persons who had been voted for to serve under the charter of the city of Lawrence. Old Ex-Governor Shannon laughed at this, but he did not understand that it was a poor political bone that Walker deemed necessary to throw to the hungry slave power.

The Governor took the stump, and everywhere in the Territory urged on the pro-slavery party the importance of granting to the actual settlers of Kansas a fair chance to vote, and also strongly recommended that the Constitution should be submitted to a direct vote of the people. Although externally appearing to act for the interest of slavery, his policy concerning the election, and his well known liberal views about submitting the Constitution, when drafted by the Convention, to the approval of the people, divided the pro-slavery party. A great number of the rank and file sided with the Governor, while the leaders of the party combined against him. Mr. Perrin, Walker's private Secretary, in a letter to the New York Times, dated Lecompton, June 3d, 1857, says: "A middle party has sprung up, who will vote with the free State party, and there is no doubt but with this party the settlement of the Kansas question must eventually rest."

Senator Wilson, of Mass., was in Kansas in the latter part of May and fore part of June, 1857. He and Walker sometimes spoke, one after the other, from the same platform.

The Lecompton Constitutional Convention, elected under Gov. Walker, Sept. 12, 1867, refused to admit the free State delegates. Gov. Robinson (free State) had been tried for treason, August 21, by Judge Cato, who charged the jury strongly against him, but they brought in a verdict of *Not Guilty*. Nearly every officer appointed by Buchanan, except *Walker* and *Stanton*, had committed, aided and encouraged *murder* in Kansas.

Although Walker refused to send troops to protect the polls on the Kansas border, the free State men were delighted when he threw out the fraudulent returns sent in from *Johnston* and *Magee* counties. This act of justice, so faithfully done by him, was bitterly censured and condemned in a letter to him from Buchanan. The administration was now bearing hard down on Walker. The *New York Day Book*, a pro-slavery sheet, demanded his removal, because he had forfeited the good opinion of the Democracy of the Territory. Buchanan, in his message of December 8th, 1857, came out against him. Senator Stephen A. Douglas, the *Chicago Times*, and *Philadelphia Press* were among his defenders. Walker became disgusted, and resigned. His resignation was accepted by Gen. Cass, December 18th, 1857.

On the day previous the bogus Legislature had agreed to submit the Lecompton Constitution to a vote of the people. Although this pro-slavery document had been in existence since September, no one (not even Gov. Walker) had been permitted to see it.

The Kansas Legislature was composed of 13 free State men and 6 democrats in the Senate, and 29 free State men and 15 Democrats in the House.

Gov. Denver was next appointed to fill Walker's place. The free State element had now become so powerful that Gen. Lane was making numerous arrests for illegal voting. The Lecompton Constitution was repudiated by several thousands of the popular vote. This news of defeat set hard on the pro-slavery party. In Congress, Keitt, of South Carolina, grabbed Mr. Grow, member of the House from Pennsylvania, by the throat. The latter knocked him down, remarking at the same time, that "no negro-driver should crack his slave whip over him." This occurred, Feb. 6th, 1858, and produced a general row in the House, which was difficult to quell.

Buchanan, chagrined at Walker's failure in Kansas, remarked, after he had sent his Kansas message into Congress, Feb. 2d, 1858, that "he would carry Lecompton through in sixty days or die."

The free State men were not only getting strong, but bold. Gov. Denver issued a proclamation against arming the militia; yet Gen. Lane kept on arming, and stigmatized Denver as a perjurer, calumniator and tyrant. This was in March, 1858. The object of arming the militia was, if the Lecompton Constitution passed Congress, to make it impossible to organize any Government under it. On the 27th of March, 1858, persons pretending to be officers of the United States army, in search of deserters, went in the dead of night to the house of Isaac Denton, on the Osage river. Mr. Denton rose from his bed and let the pro-slavery ruffians in, when he was immediately shot dead. Mr. Hedric and Mr. Davis, his neighbors, were also on the same night murdered in the same manner.

On the 30th of the same month a Constitutional Convention was sitting at Leavenworth. The Convention drew up a remonstrance addressed to the President, Congress, and the Legislatures of the different States. This instrument set forth, 1st, that the Lecompton Constitution *was not the act of the people of Kansas*; 2d, that it had been condemned by them. It was signed by Winchell, Thacher, Emery, Walden and Foster. Ex-Gov. Walker, after reading this remonstrance, in a letter to S. S. Cox, said, "If the Lecompton bill now pending in Congress pass, the odious Lecompton Constitution, born in fraud, and baptized in forgery and perjury, will be defeated by an overwhelming vote by the people of Kansas." Secretary Stanton, in a letter about the same date, said: "The Constitution has once been rejected by the people of Kansas, and why does Congress wish to send it back again to be repudiated."

Persifer F. Smith, the pro-slavery commander sent out by Jeff. Davis, under Pierce's administration, to supersede Gen. Sumner, died at Leavenworth, May 16, 1858. Only three days after, as though hell had been reinforced, Capt. Hamilton, a Missourian, with 25 armed ruffians, 17 of whom were from Missouri and 8 from Kansas, captured 11 free State men in the southern part of Kansas, and at a ravine near Fort Hamilton, placed them in a row standing, when he ordered his men to take aim and fire. They all fell at the first discharge; five were instantly killed, and five severely wounded. The murderers then went up and began to rifle their pockets. Finding one still unhurt, the Captain placed his pistol to his ear and put the ball through his head. One of the men, who had been slightly wounded, was overlooked in their great haste to escape; he worked his way back to the post and told the sad news. Many of these ruffians were personally acquainted with their victims, and murdered them because they were free State men. Campbell, Colpetzer, Ross, Stilman and Robinson, were some of the dead. Reed, a baptist preacher, Hall and Hargraves, (father and son,) were among the severely wounded. The names of the others we could not procure.

To prevent the repetition of these outrages, the free State party encouraged Capt. Montgomery to organize a sufficient force, with which he afterwards frequently made excursions into Missouri. In a little speech, this free State Captain said, " he made no war on peaceable citizens, be they pro-slavery or free State, but only on those who are devastating Kansas, and murdering peaceful citizens; neither did he allow any of his men to insult a woman."

Gov. Denver accomplished very little during his term of office. He made a treaty of peace similar to that of Shannon, but the pro-slavery party broke it by commencing indiscriminately to murder the people of Fort Scott. He resigned Sept. 21, 1858.

Buchanan, determined to make Kansas a slave State, although so often defeated, was resolved to make one more effort. On the 12th of November, 1858, he appointed Samuel Medary, formerly Editor of the Ohio Statesman, and more recently Ex-Governor of Minnesota Territory. His instructions were to prevent Kansas from sending a Constitution into Congress that winter, if possible.

A few persons said, and a great many believed, that the pro-slavery murderer, Capt. Hamilton, was instructed from Washington to commit his depredations in order that a plausible excuse could be had for making another military effort to subdue the free State men. One thing is certain, Medary had scarcely got warm in his seat when Hamilton charged the people of southern Kansas with stealing negroes. Mr. Bailey, and several other free State men, were murdered in December, and Medary made a requisition on the President for military aid.

Medary endeavored to do away with the expressive names of pro-slavery and free State men, and introduce the good old titles of Democrats and Republicans. He thought the name of Democrat would cover a multitude of sins, and perhaps it might change him from being the tool of a corrupt administration to being the choice of the people of Kansas. He became a candidate for Governor, in opposition to Charles Robinson, at the election of December 6, 1859. Hon. Abraham Lincoln was in Kansas during the canvass. It was an animated one. Medary was backed up by the administration. He had as his supporters Russell's and Waddell's teamsters, the Indian agents, and hangers on generally. Every effort was made to secure Democratic success, but it failed. Robinson was elected Governor by about 3,000 majority, and the entire Republican ticket by about the same vote. The Governor and members of Congress were the same that were elected under the Topeka Constitution of 1855 ; and Topeka, as then, now became the State Capital.

Thus bribery, forgery, perjury, arson and murder, under various pretenses, with the assistance of two corrupt administrations of the Federal Government, backed up by the slave power, seducing the weak and striking down the strong, leaving no effort untried, even unto fire and blood, to force slavery into Kansas, failed. The God of battles saw these murders and secret assassinations; the groans of the victims ascended like incense from liberty's altar, and he swore by himself that Kansas should be free.

Although Medary was overwhelmingly defeated by the people of Kansas in the December election, still, by instructions from Buchanan, he continued to stay in the Territory. The people of Kansas had chosen a Governor ; but Medary was left by Buchanan to keep up the strife, and guard and protect, with the fidelity of a watch-dog, the institution of slavery. . In February, 1860, the Kansas Legislature passed a bill prohibiting slavery in Kansas. Medary vetoed it, and on the 29th of the same month the same Legislature passed it over his veto. He had previously, by the aid of the military, cleaned out all the settlers on the Indian national lands south of Fort Scott. This was done at the commencement of winter, and hundreds of them perished from hunger and cold. Between the action of the Federal Government and its ally, Capt. Hamilton, the deaths from cold, hunger and assassination, in this part of Kansas, were frightful to contemplate.

Capt. Montgomery, as we have before stated, organized a company for the defence of the free State settlers in southwestern Kansas. Frequent charges had previously been made against him, and in 1859 he gave himself up to Gov. Medary to be tried, but no grand jury could be found in Kansas that would indict him, He finally became the terror of the slaveholders and border ruffians of southwestern Missouri. In

November, 1860, placards were extensively posted and circulated in that region setting forth that Capt. Montgomery, with a band of abolitionists, were setting free and running off all the slaves in the border counties. This was untrue; but it was the last desperate effort of a corrupt administration to revive and rally the pro-slavery element for another struggle to force slavery into Kansas.

At this time the entire slave interest in Missouri, from Gov. Stewart down, became alarmed. Stewart called out a large force of militia, and sent them to the border. The administration at Washington sent out Gen. Harney to assist Gov. Medary. Harney wanted to take the matter out of the Governor's hands, by declaring martial law; but Medary insisted that the Government troops should only be used to assist the U. S. Marshal to make arrests. Harney's object in declaring martial law was, that he could then immediately court-martial and shoot Montgomery and his party when they were captured.

It was now rumored that Montgomery was at Mound City with three hundred well armed men. Harney, fearing to make an attack on the city alone, requested the aid of Gen. Frost. With their united strength they advanced; but when they arrived they failed to find Montgomery. From this time forward all kinds of exaggerated stories and pro-slavery lies were freely circulated: Montgomery was here to-day committing depredations; to morrow he was somewhere else slaughtering the masters and stealing their slaves.

John Brown, who had suffered so much from the pro-slavery border ruffians of Missouri, understanding well the nature of the Kansas contest, concluded about this time to make a flank movement, and change his base from the Osage country of that Territory to Harper's Ferry, Virginia. As a great number of Virginians, including the son of Ex-Gov. Johnston, had come to Kansas to fight him and his cause, he thought it courtesy to return the compliment. Arrangements having been made to Brown's satisfaction, he and his company entered Maryland by way of Chambersburg, Pa., and took up their quarters in Washington county, at a house previously rented, about five miles from Harper's Ferry. The party comprised only 20 men besides Brown, the commander-in-chief; five of them were negroes. On the night of the 16th of October, 1859, these men forcibly seized the U. S. arsenal at Harper's Ferry, and held it from half past ten o'clock on Sunday night until about ten o'clock on Tuesday morning. The assault to re-capture the arsenal was made by the United States Marines, led on by Col. Harris, Lieut. Green, and Maj. Russell. Fifteen of Brown's men were killed, three wounded, and five taken prisoners. Six citizens were killed.

This was not a slave insurrection, but a continuation of the Kansas struggle. It was the first blow that the free State men struck at their old enemy outside of that Territory. Brown understood well the nature of the hideous monster, and thought he was doing God's service to beard him in his den. Physically, the magnitude of the undertaking was too great for the small means under Brown's command; but its tragical termination, and the bravery of his death, gave to liberty another martyr, and to freedom a new impulse. Although his body lies mouldering in the ground, his soul is in the Union army triumphantly marching on.

Through two presidential terms the slave power kept up the Kansas slavery agitation. Through the repeal of the Missouri Compromise, it was opened by Pierce's administration, and continued with an energy worthy of a better cause until his term of office expired. It was then passed over to Buchanan, as the life and soul of the Democratic party, and he revived, extended, and encouraged the agitation for two years in Congress under the names of Lecompton, and anti-Lecompton Democrats, then Crittenden Compromise, Montgomery-Crittenden Compromise, and then again the English bill. Thus, under the guidance of the slave power, and the treason of Pierce and Buchanan, the Democratic party became corrupted, demoralized, divided and ruined.

During Buchanan's entire term of office he refused to acquiesce in the settlement of the Kansas question. He pros-

SLAVERY OUTRAGES IN KANSAS.

tituted the Federal Government by rewarding with office those who supported his slave policy by voting for the Lecompton Constitution. Joseph Miller, of Ohio, a weak and wavering Democrat, was rewarded for his vote in favor of Lecompton with a judgeship in Nebraska; a half dozen more were similarly rewarded. But Douglas, Broderic,* Walker, Stanton and Forney, whom he could not bribe, were denounced as traitors to the Democratic party. Gov. Medary, now discovering that Buchanan was determined not to permit the Kansas question to be settled during his administration, resigned, December 20, 1860.

It was determined that this question should be the final excuse for separation and disunion. The war had commenced in Kansas, and was five years in full blast before John Brown made his raid on Harper's Ferry, and was in its seventh year before President Lincoln took his seat. The faithful historian, who seeks truth, will find slavery to have been the cause, the repeal of the Missouri Compromise an accessory before the fact, and driving freedom out of Kansas at the point of the bayonet, the exact time when the rebellion commenced.

---

* Backed up and encouraged by the administration at Washington, a combination of pro-slavery Democrats was formed in California to take the life of Senator Broderic. He boldly denounced the Lecompton fraud, and Senator Gwin, unable to cope with him in argument, gave Broderic to understand that he was anxious to fight him a duel. Broderic refused to fight until after the election. Another pro-slavery dog, by the name of Perley, also challenged him to fight. Broderic refused. Justice Terry, a Lecompton Democrat, an experienced duelist and an excellent shot, then challenged him. Broderic had previously taken this man out of the hands of the Vigilence Committee, and thus saved his life. He now saw there was a price set upon his head, and again declined; but Terry pressed the matter so hard that Broderic at last, fearing private assassination, accepted the challenge. The duel was fought September 13, 1859. Broderic fell at the first fire, pierced through the lungs, and died on the 16th. Calhoun Benner and Tom Hays were Terry's seconds, and J. H. McKibbon seconded Senator Broderic. Buchanan dreaded this powerful opponent, and the slave holders also dreaded him, and were determined to have his life. Brought up in the city of New York, and unaccostomed to the use of fire arms, he had no chance with the individual who had been pitched upon to take his life. His death was a public, political murder, for the benefit of pro-slavery principles and pro-slavery men.

Jeff. Davis, as Secretary of War under Pierce, ordered Gen. Smith to bring the Federal forces into the field to drive freedom out of Kansas. This was in 1856 ; and on the 9th of February, 1861, he is appointed commander-in-chief of the slaveholder's rebellion at Montgomery, Alabama. Ceasing to control, he determines to destroy the Federal Government.

THE SLAVEHOLDERS BECOME SAVAGES, AND COMMENCE WAR AGAINST CIVILIZATION.

South Carolina, on the 20th of December, 1860, takes the lead. The rebel chiefs, decorated in all the panoply of war, now assembled at Charleston, and joined in a war dance, stamping, yelling, and brandishing their scalping-knives and tomahawks, threatening death and universal slaughter against the tribes of the North. These demonstrations were looked upon by the South Carolina tribe as immense, and full of promise for the future. Great care was taken to send hourly reports, of the most exciting nature, from Camp Charleston, to all the other slaveholding tribes. Thus, in one of these reports, Chief Ruffian was represented as having made a great speech, in which he said : "*The independence of the Southern tribes can only be secured by the tribe of South Carolina taking the lead.*" This speech, which was made at Columbia, was represented as causing a furore of excitement among the *braves*.

Another Bull.—" Virginia and other slaveholding States may as well at once understand their position with the South Carolina tribe."

Still Another.—"The South Carolina tribe is decidedly in, earnest. There is but one voice among them, and that is for war. They have done counseling—now they act."

These fire-brands of revolution were swiftly carried in every direction by the savages, and served to excite the different tribes to join in the foul plot. As was intended, the excitement by this means soon reached the neighboring tribes. Mississippi was the first to show sympathy ; and on the 9th day of January, 1861, they agreed to send warriors to

Charleston. South Carolina has 703,812 of a tribe, and 402,541 slaves. Mississippi has 791,396 of a tribe, and 436,696 slaves.

On the 10th of the same month the tribe of Florida, numbering 140,439 souls, holding 61,753 slaves; also on the 11th, the tribe of Alabama, numbering 964,296 souls, holding 435,132 slaves, both of these tribes sent warriors to the camp at Charleston. And on the 19th of January the great and powerful tribe of Georgia, numbering 1,057,329 souls, holding 462,232 slaves, also joined the war party, and sent warriors to the great camp at Charleston. On the 26th of January the *tribe* of Louisiana, numbering 709,290 souls, holding 333,010 slaves, joined the others by sending warriors to Camp Charleston. On the 1st day of February, the tribe from the Rio Grande, Texas, numbering 602,432 souls, holding 180,682 slaves, sent warriors, and joined the other tribes in the fortunes of war.

Seven tribes had now banded together, and had a great number of warriors congregated at Camp Charleston. The other tribes appeared to be holding off.

It was not until after the seven tribes had united, that a chief was selected. On the 9th of February, 1861, Davis was, by the consent of the other chiefs, at Montgomery, Alabama, declared to be the great chief, around whom were to be gathered all the slaveholding tribes.

Thus, *South Carolina, Mississippi, Georgia, Alabama, Florida, Louisiana* and *Texas*, make seven tribes. Combined they number 4,968,994 souls, and hold 2,312,028 slaves.

It was their determination so to arrange matters, that when hostilities commenced other tribes would be brought in by the excitement. And for the purpose of getting up the war fever, Wise started for the James River, and from there he went to the Blue Ridge Country, every where urging the great men of the tribe to prepare for war. In this way all the eastern part of the country, inhabited principally by that portion of the Virginia tribe that held slaves, was worked into excitement. In the valleys and on the hills the blue smoke by day, and the red lights by night, could every where be seen; while Wise went from camp to camp, counseling the braves and training them for the conflict.

Among the tribes living east of the Blue Ridge, all peaceful pursuits were abandoned by day, and the horrors of night were increased by the howl of the wolf, the scream of the panther, and yell of the savage—all equally ravenous and thirsting for blood.

Thus *Wise*, with his eloquence, had made all things ready, and only one thing was needed, and that was some one to lead. Chief *Ruffian*, a very old man, was of the Virgina tribe, and upon his head fell the honors of commencing the work of death. *And on the morning of the 12th of April*, 1861, *at precisely* $4\frac{1}{2}$ *o'clock*, standing near the grave of Oceola, in Fort Moultrie, he fired the first gun at Sumter. This fort, although strong, contained only a force of one hundred and nine men; while the attacking force numbered above ten thousand. Thirty-three hours the little garrison held out against overwhelming numbers, when they were compelled, the fort being on fire, to surrender, and haul down the starry flag. After which was run up the Palmetto flag of South Carolina.

Now the management in putting forward Ruffian was in accordance with the programme laid down. Only five days after he commenced the attack on Fort Sumter, on the 17th of April, the tribe of Virginia joined the ignominious seven. This was a great acquisition, a very powerful tribe, numbering 1,596,079 souls, and holding 490,887 slaves; and located near and joining lands with some of the great Northern tribes, its acquisition was heralded with delight by the chiefs.

On the 6th of May, the tribe known as Arkansas, numbering 435,427 souls, and holding 111,104 slaves; also on the 7th of the same month, the tribe from the Cumberland, known as *Tennessee*, numbering 1,109,847 souls, and holding 275,784 slaves; and on the 20th of May, the tribe from Pamlico Sound, known as North Carolina, numbering 992,667 souls, and holding 331,081 slaves, joined the others.

This made eleven tribes that had embarked in the war,

numbering in all, men, women and children, 9,103,014 souls. The *slaves* held by these eleven tribes number 3,521,884. There remains four tribes, holding slaves, that have refrained, in a legislative capacity, from joining the war party. Although thousands and thousands of their braves, and many of their chiefs have gone on their own account, and are now fighting in the army of the South, yet the tribes themselves, although many of their members sympathize, have never yet joined the rebellion in force. Their names are Maryland, numbering 687,034 souls, and holding only 87,188 slaves. Missouri, numbering 1,182,317 souls, and holding only 114,965 slaves. Kentucky, numbering 1,155,713 souls, and holding 225,490 slaves. The little tribe of Delaware, numbering 112,218 souls, and holding only 1,798 slaves.

Thus, these four tribes are not in actual hostility against the North; yet the great majority of their leading men have very decided sympathies with the South. The four tribes number 3,137,282 souls, and hold only 429,441 slaves.

The condition of the country, long before President Lincoln came to Washington, was deplorable. Not only had seven States passed the ordinance of secession, and organized a Confederacy, but also many, or nearly all the forts in the slave States, had been seized on the 2d of January, 1861. Forts Pulaski and Jackson, in Savannah Harbor, Georgia, were taken possession of by the tribe in that State; the former mounting 150 guns, and cost the General Government $923,000; the latter mounting 14 guns, and cost $80,000.

On January 4th, the next day, Fort Morgan, in Mobile Harbor, was seized by the Alabama tribe. It cost the General Government $1,212,000, and mounts 132 guns; also the Arsenal at Mobile, containing 800 stand of arms, and 1,500 barrels of powder, 300,000 rounds of cartridges.

On the 9th of the same month the steamer Star of the West, while on her way to Fort Sumter, in Charleston harbor, with provisions for the starving garrison, was fired into, two shots taking effect.

On the 11th of January, Forts St. Phillips and Jackson, on

the Mississippi, and Fort Pike, on Lake Ponchartrain, and the United States Arsenal at Baton Rougue, were all taken by the Louisiana tribe.

On January 13th, Fort Barrancas, and the United States Navy Yard at Pensacola, were seized by the Florida tribe; and the United States Arsenal at Augusta, Geo., was seized by the tribe of Georgia on the 24th of January; and on the 31st of the same month, the Mint belonging to the United States, at New Orleans, was seized, with $389,000 of Government money, and $122,000 in the Sub Treasury.

The Peace Convention now commenced its sittings at Washington. How humiliating it is to read how the South spurned every offer to prevent the effusion of blood.

The Illinois and Kentucky Legislatures had previously recommended Congress to call a Convention to change the Constitution of the United States, so as to give additional guarantees to slavery. In the excitement that was raging, Virginia sent invitations to all the States, inviting them to send delegates to a Convention, to be held in Washington, D. C., on the 4th of February, 1861. Only twenty States responded; seven slave—Delaware, Virginia, Kentucky, Maryland, Missouri, North Carolina and Tennessee; thirteen free —New York, New Jersey, New Hampshire, Massachusetts, Connecticut, Rhode Island, Maine, Vermont, Pennsylvania, Ohio, Indiana, Illinois and Iowa.

This Convention (wholly unknown to the Constitution) assembled about one month after the traitors at Charleston had fired on the ship Star of the West, which was taking provision to the starving garrison at Fort Sumter. It was without legal form, and got up by traitors to gain time, and keep down the rising ire of the North. Many well-meaning men of the free States went to see what additional concessions were required to appease the wrath of the slave-drivers. These self-constituted settlers of our national difficulties, although without authority, offered to do any and everything for peace. Many of them, with tears in their eyes, went on bended knees, and implored the traitors to desist. They even went so far as to elect Ex-President John Tyler, the accessory to President Harrison's assassination, President of the Convention.

The Committee on Propositions brought in, and were ready to give their consent to add a new article to the Federal Constitution, to be composed of seven sections, to be called Article 13th.

The first section provided for a division of all the existing territory by the line of 36 deg. 30 min.

The second section was a pledge never to acquire any more, except with the concurrence of a majority of all the Senators of the slave States and all the Senators of the free States.

The third section prohibited Congress from interfering with slavery within any State, or in the District of Columbia, without the consent of Maryland; and the slaveholders therein also prohibited any interference with slavery in the Territories, and the slave trade between the slave States.

The fourth section guaranteed that the Fugitive Slave Act should everywhere be respected.

Fifth—The interests of Virginia required that the foreign slave trade should be prohibited. This section prohibited it.

The sixth section bound the United States to pay for all fugitive slaves rescued by violence.

Mr. Chase made an able speech before the Convention. He said: "Mr. President, let us not rush headlong into that unfathomable gulf. Let us not attempt this unutterable woe. We offer you a plain and honorable mode of adjusting all differences. It is a mode which, we believe, will receive the sanction of the people. We pledge ourselves here that we will do all in our power to obtain their sanction for it. Is it too much to ask you, gentlemen of the South, to meet us on this honorable and practicable ground? Will you not, at least, concede this to the country?"

On the conclusion of these remarks, the question was taken upon the proposed amendment to the Constitution, and it was rejected by the following vote, every slave State voting against it:

Ayes—Connecticut, Illinois, Indiana, Iowa, Maine, Massachusetts, New York, New Hampshire, Vermont—9.

Noes—Delaware, Kentucky, Maryland, Missouri, New Jersey, North Carolina, Ohio, Pennsylvania, Rhode Island, Tennessee, Virginia—11. The Ohio delegation voted as instructed by its Legislature.

On February 8th, the United States Arsenal at Little Rock, with 9,000 stand of Arms and 40 cannon, including Bragg's Battery, was seized by the Arkansas tribe.

February 18th, the Southern traitor, General Twiggs, having command of our main army on the frontiers of Texas, surrendered his entire force, his men being made prisoners of war, and all their arms, munitions and supplies were turned over to the enemy.

All this was done while Buchanan and his Cabinet were doing all they could to destroy and disable the Federal Government. Tousey, his Secretary of the Navy, under different pretentions, had dispersed the fleet, sending some to cruise around the coasts of China and Japan; some to the Mediterranean, and some to the West Indies, so they might rot by the action of the elements in the tropical seas. Others were sent to the coast of Africa, under the pretense of capturing slaves, until scarcely a United States war vessel could be seen in the Federal waters.

Floyd, his Secretary of War, was equally industrious, transferring from the free States all the available war material to the arsenals and forts located in the slave States. He also removed that portion of the Federal army located on and near the seaboard (where it was easy of access) far away —some to Texas, New Mexico, Arizona, Oregon, California, and other frontier stations, from which it would require a year to bring them back. Even on the 15th of November Fortress Monroe, in Virginia, was only garrisoned by eight companies of artillery; the valuable arsenal at Fayetteville, North Carolina, by one company; Fort Moultrie, in Charleston harbor, by two companies, (only eighty men); Key West fortifications by one company; Barrancas Barracks, Pensa-

DYING DAYS OF DEMOCRATIC RULE.

cola, by one company; the richly stored arsenal at Baton Rouge, Louisiana, by one company; while the New Orleans Mint, and the valuable Custom-houses in New Orleans, Charleston, Mobile and Savannah, were totally without guard. Norfolk Navy-yard, and Pensacola Navy-yard, both having millions of property, were only guarded by one hundred and twenty marines.

The first demand made of the President by the rebels, after the plot was developed, was, that no reinforcements should be sent to Southern fortresses. General Scott plead with Buchanan to throw a strong force into Fort Moultrie, as had been done in 1832; but Buchanan, instead of doing so, assured the rebels that none would be sent.

Thus the Government, betrayed, stood with both arms paralyzed; and while in this condition seven States, headed by South Carolina, one by one tore themselves away, taking seven forts, four arsenals, one Navy-yard, and the Mint belonging to the United States at New Orleans, with five hundred and eleven thousand dollars. The value of the property stolen, up to this time, is set down at twenty-seven millions of dollars; add to this the eight millions of Indian Trust Bonds stolen by Floyd, and it makes thirty-five millions of dollars.

Thus, before President Lincoln was within a thousand miles of the Capital, we find a Democratic President and Vice President, and leading Cabinet officers, all rotten with treason and besmeared with crime, a Government betrayed, robbed, bound hand and foot, bleeding and festering and festering and bleeding at every wound; with a bastard institution holding its councils and head-quarters at Montgomery, Alabama, with Davis as leader, martialing its thousands of armed foes, all eager and bent on destroying the beneficent Government they had so foully betrayed.

From there we again look back to Washington, only for a change. There we see Buchanan, the Chief Magistrate, an imbecile traitor, tottering away in disgrace, with scarcely courage enough to look back on the awful tragedy which his foul treachery, sympathy or imbecility, had shared in producing. Nearly all his cabinet officers had fled, to escape the punishment due their crimes. But Buchanan remained longest, and on the last days of his power pleasingly contemplated, with a grim-like smile which grew to a laugh, the agonizing sufferings of a wrecked and ruined country: remarking as he retired, "As George Washington was the first, James Buchanan will be the last President of the United States."

The presidential election of 1860 found the political elements in a very unsettled condition. Buchanan had given a secret pledge to the South before he received his nomination at Cincinnati (and he kept it) that the Kansas war should not be settled during his administration. The Democratic party had become demoralized. From the exalted position of defending human freedom and popular government, it became the reviler of liberty and deadly enemy of free institutions. It set aside the rights of man to make room for Calhoun's rights of the States. The popular will was to be controlled by bribery and fraud, and was only to be tolerated when it served slavery and placed Democrats in office. *Pro-slavery, disunion, anti-abolition, and a death grip on the spoils,* were the substitutes offered by Pierce and Buchanan for the Democratic principles established by Jefferson and Jackson.

At Chicago, in May, 1860, Lincoln and Hamlin received the nomination of the Republican party for the offices of President and Vice President of the United States for the ensuing four years. The 3d article in the platform adopted, contains the following: "We hold in abhorrence all schemes for disunion, come from whatever source they may." Another article stipulated that Kansas should of right be immediately admitted as a State under the Constitution, recently formed and adopted by her people, and accepted by the House of Representatives.

At Baltimore, June 22, 1860, Stephen A. Douglas and Herschell V. Johnston were nominated for the offices of President and Vice President by the Democratic party. On the next day, June 23, the disunion wing of that party nominated John C. Breckinridge and Joseph Lane for the same positions. This wing of the party proclaimed slavery national, and freedom only sectional.

In May, 1860, John Bell and Edward Everett were nominated for President and Vice President by the tail of the old Whig party, which all supposed to have died in 1852. They went in for the Constitution of the country, the Union of the States, and the enforcement of the laws.

Lincoln and Hamlin carried 17 States—180 electoral votes. Breckinridge and Lane carried 11 slave States—72 electoral votes. Bell and Everett carried 3 States—39 electoral votes. Douglas and Johnston carried Missouri and part of New Jersey—12 electoral votes.

Abraham Lincoln and Hannibal Hamlin clipped both the Douglas and Breckinridge wings of the Democratic party, and cut off the tail of Bell and Everett. Lincoln had a clear majority of 57 electoral votes over all opposition. This was a glorious triumph for the Union, a day of rejoicing for liberty, and a proud day for freedom—a day of rescue and deliverance of the General Government from treason and traitors—a day that shall add new lustre to the American name, and create joy in the hearts of millions yet unborn.

THE PLOT TO ASSASSINATE PRESIDENT LINCOLN.

Twenty men had been hired in Baltimore to assassinate the President elect on his way to Washington. The leader of this band was an Italian refugee, a barber well known in Baltimore. Their plan was as follows: When Mr. Lincoln arrived in that city, the assassins were to mix with the crowd, and get as near his person as possible, and shoot at him with their pistols. If he was in a carriage, hand grenades had been prepared, filled with detonating powder, such as *Orsini* used in attempting to assassinate Louis Napoleon. These were to be thrown into the carriage, and to make the work of death doubly sure, pistols were to be discharged into the vehicle at the same moment. The assassins had a vessel lying ready to receive them in the harbour. From thence they were to be carried to Mobile, in the seceded State of Alabama.

Gen. Scott heard of the plot, and advised with Senator Seward; and they sent Frederick W. Seward, the son of the Senator, to meet Mr. Lincoln in Philadelphia, and urge him to come to Washington in a private manner. It was late on Thursday night, February 21st, that Mr. Seward arrived in Philadelphia. He immediately went to the Continental Hotel, and communicated the facts to Mr. Lincoln. His reply was that he would fulfill his engagements in Philadelphia and Harrisburg if he should lose his life.

On the next day, 22d, (Washington's birthday,) according to promise, Mr. Lincoln raised the American flag on Independence Hall, Philadelphia. He had also accepted an invitation of the Pennsylvania Legislature to meet them that afternoon. He did so; and remained at Harrisburg until

20 minutes before 6 o'clock, that evening, when he embarked, in company with Col. Lamon, for Philadelphia, at which place he arrived at 11¼ o'clock, and took the through night train (which was a little behind time) to Washington. The party entered the sleeping car at Philadelphia, and passed through Baltimore without any one there knowing he was aboard the train. They arrived in Washington at 6½ o'clock on Saturday morning, the 23d of February. The President wore no disguise whatever, but journeyed in his ordinary traveling dress. His enemies had sworn that he should never be inaugurated; therefore it was necessary to keep a close watch on the movements of the conspirators. This was done by the aid of detectives until after his inauguration. The names of the conspirators are in the possession of responsible parties, including the President, but for wise purposes are withheld for the present.

Mr. Lincoln was inaugurated President on the 4th of March, 1861. After being introduced to the assembled crowd by Senator Baker, of Oregon, he read his inaugural address, and was then sworn in by Chief Justice Taney.

While President Lincoln and his Cabinet were engaged in sifting out and sending adrift the official traitors that surrounded Buchanan, the South was mostly occupied in getting control of all the property belonging to the General Government and arranging matters so as to become absolute masters of all the slaveholding States. The Golden Circle, and other secret military organizations, gave them great advantage in getting an organized army early into the field. They had long been drilling for the conflict which they had brought about, and which they long since had determined to settle only by the sword; their minds were made up; not wavering, but settled and determined and impatient for the strife. The free States did not dream that the plot was so extensive, or that treason was so deeply rooted and universal in the slave States. From the President down the people of the North were surprised and confounded, and for a time were unable to determine what course to pursue. While we were wavering and inclining to compromise, the South was firm and resolved to accept none. Unconditional independence was their ultimatum. Mr. Lincoln did not understand matters when, on the 15th of April, he called for only 75,000 volunteers, and commanded the rebels to return to peace in twenty days. To this small demand Gov. Magoffin, of Kentucky, Gov. Letcher, of Virginia, Gov. Harris, of Tennessee, and Gov. Jackson of Missouri, (all slave States) refused to furnish their quotas. This was an eye-opener; and Mr. Lincoln now for the first time began to realize his condition and the condition of the country. The free States began to vote money and organize armies to support the Federal cause.

While the treasonable Confederate commissioners were in Washington threatening and demanding, Pennsylvania, Massachusetts and New York were organizing and sending forward regiments. On the 18th of April the Pennsylvania volunteers reached Washington. On the same day the Massachusetts 6th regiment passed through New York on its way, and next day, while passing through Baltimore, was attacked by a pro-slavery mob. Two of its men were killed, and ten wounded. They fired into the mob, killing eleven, and wounding about thirty. The same day the New York 7th regiment left for Washington. The Governor of Maryland and Mayor of Baltimore informed the President that Baltimore was in the hands of a mob, and troops going that way to the capital would have to fight their way through. On the 3d of May Mr. Lincoln called for 42,000 three years' men. He was still loth to believe that the entire slave States were rotten with treason. The South had called for no particular number of troops, but on the 9th of May the Rebel Congress authorized Davis to accept all that offered.

The object of the war was wholly misunderstood by a great majority at the North, and is hardly yet understood by all. The South went into the contest united in relation to the cause, object, and policy of the war. The free States embarked in it, divided both as to its cause, policy to be pursued, and object to be attained. Some Generals supposed that in protecting slave property the Union could be cemented, by convincing the South that the free States did not wish to molest, but on the contrary would fight for the sacred institution. Others thought that it was not the business of the Union army to concern itself about slavery, either to protect or destroy it. Still another very powerful and intelligent class, seeing a little further, discovered slavery to be the heart of the rebellion, and that the quickest way to destroy it was to strike it where it lived. The first class loved slavery for its own sake; the second neither admired nor hated it, but thought it impolitic to meddle with it; the third despised and detested it, and saw in its downfall a fruitful victory, and a restored and happy Union, extending from the Lakes to the Gulf, and from the Atlantic to the Pacific, with a justified present and a glorious future. The first party despised the abolitionists more than they did the rebels; the second class blamed them for bringing about the war; the third, having a foundation like the rock of Gibraltar, remained firm amidst the changing storms and waves of the political sea.

Some men's judgments lie buried so deep that experience, although a great teacher, is unable to reach them. This class, with eyes wide open at noonday, will swear it is night. They invariably despise Mr. Lincoln, and admire Davis and Lee. Indeed, some of those who voted for

Lincoln, and are supposed to be high in his confidence, have even at this late day failed to discover that slavery has anything to do with the war.

Despised by the South, hated by the Democratic place-men and their dupes, counciled and suspicioned by the conservatives, and deceived by traitors in disguise, Mr. Lincoln must have been directed by divine wisdom and strengthened by its power to have grown so fast and so strong amidst such adverse surroundings.

On the 21st of July Gen. McDowell, with an organized force of 18,000 inexperienced troops, attacked Gen. Beauregard, with 27,000 rebels, at Bull Run. For ten hours the ground was hotly contested, when, without any seeming cause, a panic seized the Union army, and the entire force fled in disorder back towards the Capital. Our loss was about 500 killed and 1,000 wounded, and Beauregard had taken 1,500 prisoners. This was the first effort the disarmed and paralyzed Federal Government made to *strike back* at the traitors. It was a weak and unsuccessful stroke, and served to inspire them to new and more desperate deeds.

On the 10th of August, Gen. Lyon, with 5,200 men, at Wilson's Creek, Missouri, made an attack on McCulloch, Rains, Price and Jackson, with a combined force of 24,000 rebels. The rebel loss was greater at this battle than Beauregard had sustained at Bull Run, being 421 killed and 1,300 wounded; the Union loss was 263 killed and 721 wounded. The odds were tremendous and the contest desperate. The brave and heroic Lyon was killed while heading a charge on the enemy's lines. His troops retreated in good order to Rolla.

John C. Breckenridge had remained in Kentucky until Sept. 21. His object in so doing was to use his influence to unite that State with Jeff. Davis. On the 20th of June Gen. McClellan first took command of the troops in Western Virginia, and on the 22d of July he was placed in command of the army of the Potomac. On the 1st of November he was appointed Commander-in-chief, which office, on account of age, General Scott had resigned. On the 13th of May he commenced his advance into Virginia, and on the 17th drove the rebels across the Chickahominy. On the 23d his own army crosses the same stream, and on the 26th he takes possession of Hanover Court House, and on the 31st fights the battles of Seven Pines and Fair Oaks. On the 25th of June he commenced his Seven Days' battles before Richmond—battles of Gaines' Hill, Golding's Farm, Chickahominy, Savage Station, White Oak Swamps, and ending at Malvern Hills, July 1st. None of these battles were considered a success for the cause of the Union; yet the rebels were severely punished in many of these terrible but undecisive contests.

President Lincoln, after witnessing the disasters that had befallen McClellan, issued a call for 300,000 volunteers. On the 11th of July he

DYING STRUGGLE OF THE REBELLION. 117

appointed Gen. Halleck Commander-in-chief. He visited the shattered army of the Potomac, and had a talk with McClellan. On the 6th, Gen. Hooker, with part of the army of the Potomac, abandoned Malvern Hill. On the 16th McClellan evacuated Harrison's Landing, and on the 17th his rear-guard crossed the Chickahominy. Gen. Pope, who had been assigned to the command of the army of Virginia, on the 26th of June, now, on the 17th of July, commenced retreating towards the Potomac, and on the 30th he fought the second battle of Bull Run, was defeated, and his entire army made its retreat in the night. After 41 days of continued disaster, Pope was relieved of his command.

The rebels, taking advantage of their success against McClellan and Pope, were now threatening Washington. On Sept 2d Gen. McClellan was assigned to take command of the army for the defence of the Capital. Burnside had the day before evacuated Fredericksburg, and on the 5th Gen. Lee commenced, at the Point of Rocks, the invasion of Maryland. On the 17th the battle of Antietam was fought, after which Lee retired across the Potomac. On the 22d Presid't Lincoln issued his proviso emancipation proclamation, and on the 1st of October visited McClellan, and urged him to cross the Potomac in pursuit of Lee. On the 26th McClellan's army again began to advance, and on the 6th of November it occupied Warrenton, Va. On the 7th, after being unsuccessful, except in defence, for 470 days, and his inactive policy having cost about $1,000,000,0000, he was removed from command, and Gen. Burnside appointed to supersede him. The battle of Fredericksburg was fought by Burnside on the 13th, and on the 16th he retreated across the Rappahannock after severe loss. Bragg, who had been intrenched at Shelbyville and Tullahoma, in Tennessee, was about this time dislodged and out-generaled by Rosecrans, who, by a master stroke of policy, became possessor of the military key of the South, Chattanooga.

Except the few bright spots in the south and southwest, such as Mill Springs, Ky., Fort Henry, on the Tennessee, Fort Donaldson, on the Cumberland, Farragut at New Orleans, and the evacuations of Nashville, Corinth, and Memphis, the year 1862 was full of disaster to the Union cause. The mere mention of Virginia or Richmond was enough to to make a Union man sick.

The year 1863 commenced with Mr. Lincoln's emancipation proclamation, which declared free the slaves in all States, or parts of States or Territories then in rebellion against the General Government. This righteous, just, necessary and popular measure, and the getting rid of McClellan, was the turning point in the war. Heaven then looked down and smiled upon the cause of the Union, and the very next day, under Gen. Rosecrans, gave us a great victory at Stono River, with trifling loss. Gen. Bragg, who commanded the rebels, lost 14,560 men, the greater portion of which were killed. On the 8th a great victory was obtained at Springfield, Mo., and on the 9th Col. Ludlow succeeded in exchanging about 20,000 rebel prisoners for the same amount of our men. On the 11th we captured Fort Arkansas and Fort McClernard; our loss was only 1,000, while that of the rebels was over 5,000, with all their arms and supplies. On the 25th the first colored regiment was organized at Port Royal, South Carolina.

On the 26th Gen. Hooker succeeded Burnside in command of the army of the Potomac; and on the 29th Gen. Banks promulgated the emancipation proclamation in New Orleans. On the 26th of February the Indian Cherokee National Council repeals the secession ordinance, and forever abolishes slavery in their tribe. On the 10th of March the 1st South Carolina colored regiment captured Jacksonville, Florida, and on the 14th the mighty Farragut moved his Mississippi fleet past Port Hudson, on the way to Vicksburg. On the 1st of April he passed the Grand Gulf batteries with small loss. On the 16th Admiral Porter's fleet passed the Vicksburg batteries, losing only one transport and no men. On the 28th of April, Gen. Hooker, with the army of the Potomac, crossed the Rappahannock, and on the 30th of April Gen. Grant's army landed near Port Gibson, Mississippi, and on the 1st of May fought the battle of Port Gibson, and commenced marching on Vicksburg. On the 2d Hooker fought the battle of Chancellorville, a hotly contested fight. Stonewall Jackson, one of the most successful rebel Generals, was wounded, and died on the 10th inst. On the 6th Hooker retreated across the Rappahannock, but Lee was unable to pursue. On the 3d the colored South Carolina regiment returned from the Cambahee river raid, bringing with them 800 slaves and destroying over $2,000,000 worth of rebel property. On May 13th Yazoo City, Mississippi, was captured by our gun-boats, and rebel property destroyed amounting to over $2,000,000.

On the 15th Gen. Grant defeated Pemberton at Edward's Ferry, and on the 16th drives him to Big Black river. On the 17th Pemberton retreated towards Vicksburg with great loss. On the 18th Gen. Grant invests Vicksburg. On the 21st the rebels offer to surrender Vicksburg if they are permitted to march out. Gen. Grant gives no conditions. On the 27th Gen. Banks assaults Port Hudson without success; great bravery was displayed by the colored troops under his command. On the 28th Boston sent out the first colored regiment that went from the North. June 6th the negro troops defeated the rebels at Miliken's Bend. On the 15th Lee marches into Maryland with 100,000 troops. On the 28th Gen. Hooker was superseded by Gen. Meade. On the 30th the rebel outworks were breached at Vicksburg. On July 1st the battle of Gettysburg commenced, and continued with varied success until the 3d, when a great victory was won by Gen. Meade. Twenty-three thousand

DYING STRUGGLE OF THE REBELLION.

of the rebels, killed and wounded, were left on the field, and 6,000 prisoners fell into our hands. Lee retreated at night towards the Potomac. On the 4th Gen. Grant obtained his immortal victory at Vicksburg, capturing the entire rebel army, 31,720 men, with all their arms and equipments, and 234 guns. About the same time Port Hudson surrendered to Gen. Banks 7,000 prisoners and 40 pieces of artillery. An understanding was had, that if Lee was successful in Maryland his friends were to rise in the city of New York. Chagrined at his defeat, and also mortified at Gen. Grant's great triumph at Vicksburg, a pro-slavery riot broke out on the 13th, killing negroes, burning the colored Orphan Asylum, and killing peaceable citizens. They were finally subdued on the 16th, after many of them had been killed. On the 26th John Morgan, with his entire command, was captured near New Lisbon, Ohio, while making a daring rebel raid, (Morgan has since been killed in Kentucky.) John B. Floyd died at Abingdon, Va., Aug. 27th. October 17th President Lincoln calls for 300,000 more volunteers. Nov. 24th, capture of Lookout Mountain, in Tennessee, Gen. Hooker fighting above the clouds.

God waited until the nation resolved to be just before he gave it success. You may search history in vain to find such a series of victories as those that followed the commencement of 1863. Battles which in their magnitude would have appalled all Europe were fought, and victories made fruitful for the Union cause, not only in the positions gained, but in the numbers of the enemy slain; which numbered, in less than 125 days, over 50,000, while those taken prisoners in the same length of time amounted to over 100,000 more. Since the commencement of Mr. Lincoln's presidential term, Russia has emancipated her slaves, and at a great meeting held July 9, 1864, at Geneva, Switzerland, patriotic resolutions were passed, applauding his emancipation policy. The good and wise of all countries, from the confines of Russia to half-civilized Japan, endorse and sustain it.

Since Gen. Grant, as Lieutenant General, has taken command of all the armies, and especially assumed command of the army of the Potomac, there has been a series of successful strategic movements, in which Lee has been out-generaled, surprised, and forced to come out from behind breastworks and fight or abandon his fortifications. Grant holds the rebellion by the throat; and Gen. Sherman in his great campaign through the center of the Confederacy, has slain about 50,000 traitors, and captured over 150 guns, and has at last taken the heart out of the monster in the capture of Atlanta. Farragut who, in 1862, illuminated the Mexican Gulf, and lit up the Mississippi with the flame of his guns, has gone with his illuminators into the dark bay of Mobile. The forts for the defence of the city are already captured, and the fall of the city itself is only a question of a few days time.

Since the President issued his emancipation proclamation, we have, with few exceptions, had almost uninterrupted success. Slavery is abolished in the District of Columbia. Maryland has become civil, and has also abolished slavery. Delaware has done the same. Missouri, that was overrun with treason, has also passed an act of emancipation. Louisiana has been reclaimed from the hand of the usurper, and has done likewise. Western Virginia has done the same. Tennessee has bid good-bye to the rebels, and, with Arkansas, is determined to come into the Union free. Georgia is now beginning to look up; the storm is passing over her, and in a few more weeks she will be out of danger. In North Carolina, South Carolina, Florida, Texas, Mississippi, Alabama, and Virginia, large portions of each and all of these States are wrested from the grasp of the spoiler. Since Jan. 1st, 1863, sufficient territory has been retaken from the rebels to form a country larger than the British Empire.

Mr. Lincoln was unanimously re-nominated by the Union Convention that assembled at Baltimore on the 7th of June, for a second term of office. No Convention ever yet assembled in the United States, that so completely represented the will and wants of the American people. We predict that he will carry almost every State, entitled to an electoral vote for President, in November, 1864. To change the policy of the General Government, every man of reflection sees disaster, disgrace, and ruin to the cause of the Union. With the reëlection of Abraham Lincoln of Illinois, and Andrew Johnson of Tennessee, the Union will virtually be restored. These are the only Union candidates, and they will receive the undivided support of every Union man.

The embarrassing circumstances which surrounded Mr. Lincoln during the commencement of his present term, the energy by which he overcame all obstacles, and his undying devotion to the cause of his country, entitles him, like our first Presidents, to a second term. With this will come a restoration of our glorious Union, and an honorable and lasting peace. Having finished the great work so ably commenced by the early Fathers, his well earned fame will enter immortality in company with Washington.

THE LAST DESPERATE SCHEME AND DEATH STRUGGLE OF THE SLAVE POWER.—FACTS FOR THE AMERICAN PEOPLE, AND FOOD FOR REFLECTION FOR EVERY MAN WHO VOTES FOR PRESIDENT OF THE UNITED STATES OF AMERICA IN NOVEMBER, 1864.

The South, finding that separation and independence could not be won by the sword, have, by the advice of the slave power, resorted to the old game. For this purpose agents were sent to Canada, to dictate a platform, and secure a candidate for Vice President at the Chicago Democratic Convention, of August the 30th. This was all they expected; it was all they desired. The peace platform was to be held up to their weakened and disheartened Southern brethren as a gleam of hope. By this means they expect to be able to hold out until after the presidential election, although their already desperate efforts have, in the language of Gen. Grant, "robbed both the cradle and the grave," and in their own language, started the blood with the sweat. In this desperate condition they needed a new and powerful stimulas to keep up their courage for a short time longer. This they got in the platform adopted at Chicago—it promised that hostilities should immediately cease. The slave power also claimed the candidate for Vice President; and in this they demanded a *reliable man*, one that would be equivalent to Jeff. Davis himself. This they secured in the nomination of *Pendleton* of Ohio. With the platform to induce the South to hold out a little longer, and Pendleton to occupy a similar position as did John Tyler in 1840—with this hellish plot secretly arranged, they hold out to the war Democrats the treacherous, blood-stained hand of the expiring slave power. The leaders, blinded by a love for office, fail to discover the deep-laid scheme, grasp with joy the hand of the monster, which in his exhausted condition is already palsied with weakness and growing cold with death; and, in order that this demon may survive, agree to make a second Harrison of Gen. McClellan. Who can fail to see that if he should be so unfortunate as to be elected, the slave power would, by his assassination, secure disunion and eternal separation. Is any man so foolish as to suppose that in such a position his life would be worth a straw?

WHY DO THE SLAVEHOLDERS DETEST THE UNION?

Claiming the right of *secession* and *revolution* is the only means to secure a separation from the free States.

But why wish to separate? Let the Northern people cease to *sympathize*, and open their *eyes, ears* and *understandings* to a realization of what the *South demands*, and why it demands it.

They, the rebels, demand an entire separation of the slave States from the free States on the line of slavery; and the numerous bloody battles already fought show boldness and determination on their part to secure it. *But what peculiar interest in the South demands the separation?* What portion of the Southern people, and what are their occupations in life, who for years have been crying, "D—n the Union?"

It is not the mercantile interest. The merchants of the South, as a class, have everything to lose, and nothing to gain, by a destruction of the Union. Neither is it the mechanical interest; the mechanics of the South have never manifested any dissatisfaction towards the Union. Neither have the boating or railroad interests anything to expect by its destruction, except complications in the carrying trade by insults and delays from custom-house officers, and increased taxation; they are not opposed to the Union. Religion of every kind and creed, without a single favorite, are all respected and protected alike, each and all enjoying the glorious privilege of worshipping God at their own time and place, and in their own way. It is not the four millions of poor, disfranchised, oppressed and degraded slaves that are scattered over the South who are rising up against, and determined to destroy the Union; no, no, it is not these.

Who, then, is engaged in this foul plot? It was commenced, and is continued. *by those wicked traffickers in human flesh, the slaveholders,* WHO, FAILING TO CONTROL, HAVE DETERMINED TO DESTROY THE UNION.

Now for the *slaveholder's* testimony as to why they are in arms:

The *Richmond Enquirer* vindicates the war on the ground that "the experiment of universal liberty has failed. The evils of free society are insufferable and impracticable in the long run. It is everywhere starving, demoralized and insurrectionary. Policy and humanity alike forbid the extension of its evils to new peoples and coming generations. THUS FREE SOCIETY MUST FALL and give way to SLAVE SOCIETY, a social system old as the world, and universal as man."

Another witness—Dr. Palmer, the moral mouth-piece of the slaveholders, preaching at New Orleans, said: "The providential trust of the South is to perpetuate the institution of *domestic slavery* as now existing, with freest scope for its natural development." We must, says the Doctor, "lift ourselves to the highest moral ground, and proclaim to all the world *that we hold this trust from God,* and in its occupancy are prepared to stand or fall."

Another witness—Alexander Stephens, the Vice President of the slaveholder's government, in a speech at Savannah, Georgia, March 12th, 1861, said: "That African slavery was the immediate cause of the late rupture and present revolution. Jefferson, in his forecast, had anticipated this as the rock on which the old Union would split. The prevailing opinion entertained by him, and most of the leading statesmen at the time of the formation of the old Constitution, was, that the enslavement of the African was in violation of the law of nature—that it was wrong in principle, *social, moral* and *political. Our new Government is founded on directly the opposite idea,* and is the first in the history of the world based on the great truth that the negro is not equal to the white man; that slavery is his natural and normal condition. Thus the stone rejected by the first builders is become the chief stone in the corner of our new edifice. Negro slavery is but in its infancy; we must increase and expand it. Central America and Mexico are all open to us."

At a public meeting held in Charleston, South Carolina, on the 17th of December, 1861, one of the speakers remarked: "The knell of this Union has been sounded, and it must go down, if it has to go down, in a stream of blood, and in a multitude of human sufferings. Three thousand millions of property (meaning slaves) is involved in this question. That Union of which so many speak in terms of laudation, its *virtues,* its spirit has forever fled. It is now a dead carcass, stinking in the nostrils of the South."

Howell Cobb, of Georgia, says: "There is, perhaps, no solution of the great problem of reconciling the interests of labor and capital, so as to protect each from the encroachments and oppressions of the other, so simple as slavery. *By making the laborer himself capital, the conflict ceases and the interests become identical.*"

A Curious and Explanatory Relic.—On Barnwell's Island, South Carolina, at the house of Mr. Prescott, were found his private papers. Rebels often run at the approach of the Union army. This traitor fled in such haste that even his private correspondence was left behind. Years after he wrote the communication calling out this letter, he was a good Democrat. In fact James Buchanan thought him so worthy as to have him as Assistant Secretary of State. The letter was written by one Garnet, then a member of the Virginia Convention, sitting to revise its Constitution, and dated May 3d, 1851.

Garnet says: "In case of South Carolina seceding, I think the Federal Government would use force, commencing with a blockade of Charleston. If you could only force the blockade, and bring the Government to direct force, *the feeling in Virginia would be very great.* Eastern Virginia is strongly in the right to secede, and is with Carolina, but the West has only 60,000 slaves to 494,000 whites; *there is the rub.* Members from this portion of the State talk strange, and I have been pained to hear them. In this body I have *apprehensions*, as well as *hopes*. You will object to the term *Democrat*. Democracy, in its original philosophical sense, *is indeed incompatible with slavery* and the whole system of Southern society. If the General Government should succeed, Southern civilization (slavery) is gone."

One more witness, and, as Lawyers say, we rest.

The *Southern Literary Messenger*, Richmond, Va., says: "Any man who does not love slavery for its own sake, as a divine institution, who does not worship it as the corner-stone of civil liberty, who does not adore it as the only possible condition on which a republican form of Government can be erected, and who does not in his inmost soul wish to see it extended over the whole earth as a means of reformation, second in dignity, importance and sacredness only to the Christian religion—he who does not love slavery with this love, is an abolitionist."

The first witness, the *Richmond Enquirer*, sets forth the objects of the war made by the slaveholders to be the total destruction of liberty, alleging that it is a monstrous evil that should not go down to future generations.

Then we are told by the second witness, Dr. Palmer, "that slavery is a Providential trust, and he calls on slaveholders everywhere to proclaim to all the world *that they hold this trust from God.*" Did ever man hear such blasphemy? Claiming that God has empowered them to establish markets and make merchandise of immortal souls, wallowing in the sweat and drinking the blood of those for whom Christ died.

Then Stephens, high in authority, the third witness, says: "the war was commenced by and in the interest of slavery. He also admits that all the leading statesmen who lived at the time, and helped to frame the old Constitution, believed slavery to be wrong; they rejected it as being unworthy to be inserted. But, says Stephens, "the stone that the builders rejected has become the chief one in the corner of our new edifice."

The fourth, Cobb, says the only way to subdue the irrepressible conflict going on between capital and labor, *is to make slaves of all laborers everywhere;* then, he says, the conflict will cease. Seward only proclaimed that there was a conflict going on between free and slave labor, but Cobb goes deeper and places it between capital and *labor*. How would some of these free laborers of the North like to have some Democratic Southerner buy them and hold them as slaves? Is that Democracy? De Bow's Review, published at New Orleans, Vol. XXV, for December, 1858, page 663, advocates the enslaving of the white race. He says: " To say the white race is not the *true and best slave race* is to contradict all history. Too much liberty is the great evil of our age, and the vindication of slavery the best corrective."

Reader, if you refuse to swallow and believe all these unnatural, treasonable sentiments, you are then branded with the horrible name of *abolitionist*.

We are often surprised that slavery should so hate its own offspring. Abolitionists did not create slavery; but who has the hardihood to deny that slavery has made every Abolitionist now in America? However obnoxious the child may be to the parent, it is a legitimate offspring, and not the unwilling production of a rape. And as it required slavery to produce abolitionists, so it required slavery to excite hatred to free society and free government, which has terminated in dreadful civil war. In the language of Calhoun, " It is the only question of sufficient magnitude to bring about the destruction of the Union."

SLAVERY.

> The highest card in the deck of sin,
> Controlling all the evil pack within;
> It's high in every game of human vice—
> In murder, too, it loads the dice.
> Kings, Queens come first, then navy Jack,
> But this card played secures the pack;
> By color cheats and holds the game,
> While Hoyle proclaims the suits the same.
> Condemn not color—oh, man, be wise—
> God made all shades beneath the skies.
> The voice of nature, whispering man be free,
> Cries slavery's death in every living tree.

By looking into the ancient histories of those countries that held slaves, we find that their mode of maintaining slavery was by *tortures* and *death*. But as America is the land of invention, perhaps some inventive genius has convinced the Almighty that a better mode is by doing violence to the human mind. Thus by Act of Assembly of Louisiana, passed in March, 1830, "all persons who shall teach or cause to be taught any slave in this State, to read or write, shall, on conviction thereof, be imprisoned not less than one or more than twelve months."

In Georgia, in 1829, it was enacted, "if any slave, negro, or free person of color, or any white, shall teach any other slave or negro, or free person of color to *read* or *write*, either writen or printed characters, the said free person of color, or slave, shall be punished by fine and whipping, or fine or whipping, at the discretion of the Court; and if a white person so offending, he, she, or they, shall be fined not more than $500, and a term in the County Jail, at the discretion of the Court"

Virginia, according to the Code of 1846 : "Every assembly of negroes for the purpose of instruction in reading or writing, shall be an unlawful assembly. Any Justice may issue his warrant to any officer or other person, requiring him to enter any place where such assembly may be, and seize any negro therein; and he or any other Justice may order such negro to be punished with stripes. If a white person assemble with negroes for the purpose of instructing them to read or write, he shall be imprisoned in jail, not exceeding six months, and fined not exceeding $100."

In 1834, South Carolina passed an act as follows : " If any person shall hereafter teach any slave to read or write, or shall aid in assisting any slave to read or write, or cause or procure any slave to be taught to read and write, such person, if a free white person, shall be fined $100, and imprisoned not more than six months. Slaves and free persons of color, shall receive not exceeding fifty lashes, and fined not exceeding $50."

In Alabama, "any person who shall attempt to teach any free person of color, or slave, to spell, read or write, shall, upon conviction, be fined not less than $200, and not to exceed $500."

Other slave States have similar enactments, but the foregoing are deemed sufficient to show to what lengths this barbarous rascality has been carried. The ancients never got so low in crime; they never dreamed of fettering the mind.

"The slave youths of promising genius," says Gibbon, the Roman historian, "were instructed in the arts and sciences, and almost every liberal profession and industrial pursuit suited to the necessities of Roman society." Thus the education of slaves was not prohibited by the Roman Government. The same is true of society in the middle Ages. Education elevated the slave in his social condition, and opened a way to emancipation.

Congreve's Politics of Aristotle, page 496, says: "The only true analysis to the slavery of Greece and Rome, is to be found in that which is still prevalent in Asia, where the evils of West India or American slavery are wholly unknown, and the relation of master and slave are accepted by both in Aristotle's words, 'at once light, and for the common interests.' On the other hand, if we seek for an analogy in ancient times to modern slavery, we may find one in the Catifiendia of the Roman nobles, or what may be termed the Corn Plantations of Sicily. The population there was slave, and there was no check to the misuse of their power by the agents or masters who superintended them, and there was no intercourse, no sense of connection to soften the inherent hardships of their condition. They rebelled once and again; and there was danger lest their revolt should spread—lest throughout the Roman world the slave population should feel that it had a common cause."

Aristotle's opinion, was, "that there ought be held out to the slave the hope of liberty as the reward of his service. Thus by a gradual infiltration, the slave population might pass into the free." It did so at Rome through the intermediate stage of freedom, and the position of freedmen at Rome in the later Republic, and even more under the Empire, was such that the prospect of reaching it must have been a great inducement to the slaves to acquiesce in their present lot.

De Tocqueville says: "The slave among the ancients belonged to the same race as his master; and he was often the superior of the two in education and instruction." Thus hardly any similarity existed between ancient and modern slavery. The former were educated, at least many of them, and had no peculiar dress to distinguish them from their masters; and many of them, naturally and by acquisition, were his superiors. But American slavery is very different. *First*, the slaves are of a different race. *Second*, they are a different color. The tradition of slavery dishonors the race, and the peculiarities of the race perpetuate the tradition of slavery. *Third*, American slavery not only controls the body, but aims to obliterate the mind of the slave. And taking advantage of all these peculiarities, the South has stepped beyond everything heretofore known on earth or in *hell*, to secure the degradation of an entire race.

Well might Jefferson remark: " Can the liberties of the nation be thought secure when we have removed the only basis— a conviction in the minds of the people, that these liberties are the gift of God? That they are not to be violated but with his wrath. *Indeed, I tremble for my country when I reflect that God is just;* that his justness can not sleep forever; that considering numbers, nature, and natural means, only a revolution of the wheel of fortune, an exchange of situation, is among possible events, that it may become probable by supernatural interference. The Almighty has no attribute which can take side with us in such a contest."

What attribute of Almighty God would allow him to take the side of the oppressor? *We ask* only, and the answer settles the argument as to which side will succeed. Sunk far below the civil law, the words of the Roman poet concerning the poor *Plebian*, with a few alterations, belong to the American slave—

> Only leaving the poor negro his single tie to life,
> The sweet, sweet love of daughter, of sister, and of wife.
> The gentle speech, the balm for all his vexed soul endures,
> The kiss in which he half forgets even such a yoke as yours;
> Still let the maiden's beauty swell the father's heart with pride,
> Still let the bridegroom's arms enfold an unpolluted bride.
> Spare him the inexpiable wrong, the unnatural shame,
> That turns his human heart to steel, the white man's blood to *flame*.
> Lest when his latest hope is fled, you taste of his despair,
> And learn by proof, in some wild hour, how much the wretched *dare*.

We have, in the body of this work, established the fact that the Southern slaveholders and their Nothern abettors were the sole originators of the terrible war now raging. We will close the volume with James Madison's opinion, as set forth in the 2d vol., page 787 of *Benton's Thirty Years in the Senate*. Benton says "Mr. Madison was a Southern man, but his Southern home could not blind his mental vision as to the origin, design, and consequences of the slavery agitation. He gave to that agitation a *Southern origin*, to that design a disunion end, to that end disastrous consequences, both to South and North."

Printed in Great Britain
by Amazon